Dear Laughing Motorbyke

Letters from Women Welders
of the Second World War

Dear Laughing Motorbyke

Edited and with an introduction
by Margaretta Jolly

Scarlet Press

Published by Scarlet Press
5 Montague Road, London E8 2HN

British Library Cataloguing in Publication Data
A catalogue record for this book is available from
the British Library
ISBN 1 85727 004 5 pb
     1 85727 014 2 hb

Designed and produced for Scarlet Press by
Chase Production Services, Chadlington, OX7 3LN
Typeset from the author's disk by
Stanford DTP Services, Northampton
Printed in the EC by J.W. Arrowsmith, Bristol

Long years ago, there were eight welders –
One of them, was me.
We worked for Mr Pearson, in
Sheffield-by-the-sea!
Our boss's lovely daughter Val,
As stream-lined as a Jag,
Taught us how to put 'runs' down
And hammer off the slag.
Mishaps – we had many,
In our early training days,
Like Alice, throwing oil, the day
Our curtains were ablaze!!!
We'd 'flashes', burns, and blistered feet,
Slagholes, by the score,
As we fused our welding rods –
Sweating in every pore.
Our efforts – they were not in vain –
We welded Churchill Tanks.
To Val, and Mr Pearson,
Our very grateful thanks.

© Leonora Agnes Helme, 1984

Contents

Foreword

Penny Summerfield, Professor of Women's History, Lancaster University

In 1985, Dorothy Sheridan discovered, as she meticulously sorted through the numerous boxes of the Mass-Observation Archive, a collection of letters written in 1942 by some Yorkshire women welders to their trainer. Dorothy generously shared the find with me when I was visiting the Archive to research women in the Second World War. We responded with fascination as much to the style and tone of the letters (one of which opens 'Dear Little Glamour Girl, Heart Throb No.1'), as to the wartime social history they revealed.

We recognised the collection as unique, a treasure trove, which would be of enormous interest if we could in some way make it publicly available. We both quoted briefly from the letters in the publications on which we were working at the time: a few short extracts appear in the book I wrote with Gail Braybon, *Out of the Cage, Women's Experiences in Two World Wars* (London, Pandora, 1987), and Dorothy included two complete letters in her book, *Wartime Women, a Mass-Observation Anthology* (London, Heinemann, 1990). But we knew that the 52 letters deserved much more than this. We toyed with the idea of jointly writing a publication based on them, framed by the problematic of women crossing the gender boundary to weld in wartime. To pave the way, Dorothy traced eight of the eleven writers of the letters and the woman trainer, Valentine Morche, with whom they were corresponding in 1942. We were encouraged not only by the fact that so many of the welders were alive but also by the warm response to our interest. They were intrigued to hear that their letters had been preserved, and willing to co-operate in some sort of project based on them. We explored with a TV producer, Sharon Goulds, of Television History Workshop, the possibility of making a documentary film about the welders, which sadly did not come off. I went to visit and to record interviews with four of the women. But aside from the problems of obtaining funds to support the project, neither Dorothy nor I were entirely confident that our social-historical approach could do justice to the letters and their writers. In particular it seemed unlikely to capture, let alone explain, the sheer pleasure of reading the letters, an entertainment value evidently intended at the time and undiminished today.

Margaretta Jolly was researching letter-writing as a literary genre at the University of Sussex, home of the Mass-Observation Archive, in the early 1990s. She came to the welders' letters equipped with intellectual and analytical insight which Dorothy and I did not have. She breathed new life into the project, and, as one of the welders might have put it, has 'brought forth fruits'. She shows us in the following pages how to read the letters, not only as windows on the history of wartime class and gender relationships and identities, for which they remain invaluable, but perhaps more importantly as examples of working-class women's creative writing. We are introduced to ways of understanding the letters, including (or especially) their unorthodox spellings, idiosyncratic punctuation, baroque turns of phrase, and fragmentary and incomplete narratives. Her insights enormously deepen our capacity to appreciate the writing. Margaretta enables us to recognise it, among other things, as confession, as an equivalent to journal writing, as sexual 'self-making', and as a form of flirtation. She also provides us with a reflexive account of her experiences as editor, in terms of the meanings both of the process and of the end result. By putting the letters together she has re/created a synthesis which only their recipients (Valentine, and through her the Mass-Observers) and not their authors experienced previously, but which is now publicly available. And she provides us with not only an immensely rich set of accounts of wartime life and female friendship, but also an analysis of the multiple relationships in play (and at play) in the 55-year history of the creation of this collection. I am confident that others will enjoy it as much as I have done.

Acknowledgements

This book has been a collective project at every stage and collaboration has been a distinctive pleasure. First and foremost, I owe special thanks to Agnes Helme, Valentine Morche, Emily Castle, Ethel and John Kergon, Alice Burden, Dorothy Adams, Joan Baines, Stephanie Buckley and John Helme, who encouraged me to publish their or their families' letters. Their conversations and memories made this much more than an academic project, bringing ideas alive and generating new friendships and correspondences. I also owe incalculable thanks to Dorothy Sheridan, Mass-Observation Archivist and Penny Summerfield, of the University of Lancaster, who originally saw the special interest of the letters and began the process of interpretation and publication. They were central to the book's final realisation. Their stimulating ideas not only about this history of women during the war but the importance and ethics of oral history have also been crucial to my development as an editor. Joy Eldridge at the Mass-Observation Archive was immensely supportive both practically and personally. Roz Platt and Martha Pratt had already done the difficult tasks of transcribing and typing up the original manuscripts. Sharon Goulds from Television History Workshop also worked to introduce the letters and their writers to a wider audience.

I also wish to thank Jo Stanley for prompting me to be creative about history, Karen Adler, Karin Voth Harman, Jacquetta Morris and Andrea Hammell for their dedication to reading drafts, my parents for their endless support and Anne Nyssen for telling me about working as a woman welder today. John Hudson at David Brown's Archive was also most helpful in contributing to my knowledge of the factory. I would also like to thank Avis Lewallen, my editor at Scarlet Press, for her enthusiasm. This book is dedicated to Ilse Singer, whose friendship and wisdom have been a constant guide during the years in which it has been in the making.

The author and publisher wish to thank the following for permission to reproduce from copyright material: the Trustees of the Mass-Observation Archive at the University of Sussex, the Trustees of the Imperial War Museum and the *Daily Mirror*. We would also like to thank John Helme and Valentine Morche for supplying their photographs.

Preface

The letters in this book date from 1942, in the middle of the war years. Valentine Pearson, a young woman working as a welding instructor in the burgeoning munitions industry, trained two groups of women to weld that year. Her trainees wrote her a lavish bundle of thank-you letters that ranged from updates on their new jobs as welders to business queries to confessions of unexpected, budding friendship – and the roguish stories of women in a world at war.

Valentine sent the letters early in 1943 to Mass-Observation, an organisation which aimed to record observations by volunteers in all walks of life. The letters were filed and lay undisturbed until 1985, when Dorothy Sheridan, the Mass-Observation Archivist, discovered them and began the process of tracing their writers. She succeeded in contacting ten of the twelve welders and also tracked down Valentine, who had emigrated to Canada after the war. Ideas began to germinate about publishing the letters and their story. In 1989, Penny Summerfield of the University of Lancaster, a historian who specialises in the history of women during the Second World War, went to interview some of them about their experiences as wartime welders. They were also interviewed by Television History Workshop.

In 1994, I began a second set of interviews, including a three-day marathon one with Valentine. The result is this collection. In the interests of clarity, I have regularised spelling, punctuation, grammar and layout. I have, however, left indications of style where I could, such as idiosyncratic punctuation or capitalisation. I have also kept the original spelling and punctuation in the citations in my introduction, for readers who are interested in the critical value of the texts.

Inevitably, these have been somewhat subjective decisions. In my view, editing is always subjective to a degree, and to that extent is a creative as well as critical task, with the responsibilities that must bring. My reasoning has been that these were private letters, not intended for a public readership. Clarification of their texts has seemed the fairest way to present them to people who will read with interest in a past time that was once the lively present.

Introduction

'The balance of power rests in women's hands. Literally. Behind the whine of sawmills and roar of blast furnaces, the hammer of arsenals and thunder of machine shops – in shipyards, factories, foundries, slaughterhouses, and laboratories – women are manipulating the machinery of war' (Bradley 1944: 193). During the Second World War, popular images of turbaned and dungareed women munitions workers were perceived to signify dramatic change in women's roles. Perhaps the best-known icon was the American illustrator Norman Rockwell's 'Rosie the Riveter', flexing her muscle for the war effort, and the British equivalent, the portrait of Ruby Loftus at her lathe, by the official war artist Laura Knight. Today many still see women's entry into paid work, especially men's work, during the war as a radical challenge to the gender hierarchy, aptly signified by the many reprints of 'Rosie' as the epitome of the proud, liberated woman.[1]* Was the war a time of greater freedom for women? Did it prefigure or even inaugurate the women's liberation movement that was to flower 25 years later? This book takes up this question through the story of a group of women at the heart of this social experiment, women who worked as welders. What makes their story so unusual is not only that they recorded it in letters, but that their letters survived.

Two groups of women went to Sheffield in 1942 to learn to weld. There they were trained by Valentine Pearson (later Morche), one of the few women who worked as a welder before the war. When they returned to their factories, they wrote to Valentine to thank her and keep her in touch with their new jobs as welders in their home-town factories. These are the letters that are collected in this book. The first section of the book contains the letters of Helena Varley, Joan Baines, Dorothy Adams and Violet Jessop, written from David Brown's foundry in Penistone, Yorkshire. The next three sections comprise the letters of a larger group of women from

* The notes for the Introduction are on pages 161–7.

Huddersfield, who were working at Hopkinsons factory, welding tanks, bridges and bombs. They were Agnes Helme, Amy Hargate, Emily Castle, Eleanor Hardcastle, Enid Hiley, Jenny and Ethel Kergon. (Three letters from Ethel's fiancé, John Kergon, are also included.) Most of these women wrote for several months after their return from their training in Sheffield, but Agnes and Amy corresponded with Valentine until their deaths.[2]

The letters in this book, hastily set down without a thought for posterity, offer us a rare glimpse into the special experiences of working women during the war. The women write of welding with a critical yet excited eye. They also write of their sexual and emotional experiences. They reveal that the war was a time in which women's struggles, as daughters, lovers, wives and mothers, were no different and indeed sometimes worse, than before, despite the media talk of women's 'liberation'. At the same time, they show what could be enjoyed in the upheaval of the war. As I shall explore in the next part of this introduction, the letters thus challenge histories of the war that are more usually told from the perspective of men and the middle classes.

The letters not only refigure conventional histories of the war. They also refigure what we think of as war writing. They do not conform to the public 'blatancy and boom' of wartime propaganda, nor even to the kinds of war letters that are usually published: those of homesick or dutiful male soldiers.[3] They suggest other aesthetic qualities – a formal intimacy, the sharp detail of the everyday, the turns of a private performance both sarcastic and affectionate. In these ways, they demand literary as well as historical reading. I explore this in terms of letter writing as a popular art and argue that they exemplify the necessity to broaden the too often narrow terms in which literary value is defined.

What was the relationship between Valentine and her trainees that provoked such creativity? We can only surmise from this half of the correspondence, for Valentine's letters were not saved. Yet two opposing themes stand out. On the one hand, there is the breezy acquaintance of middle-class teacher and working-class student. On the other hand, there is the mutual support of women working in a traditionally male domain. From these writers' point of view, it is clear that the much-heralded breakdown of the class structure during the war was more fiction than reality, yet there is a spark of identification that illuminates the exchange in unexpected ways. The letter form thus brings to the fore the questions that lie at the heart of contemporary feminism: what connects women? What are our common interests and experiences? What divides us and defines our differences?

The letters' answers to these questions depend in part upon the terms upon which they were collected and preserved. Their survival is not only a story in itself, but a case study of the politics of writing history. Here letters written by working-class women have been preserved and published by middle-class women. This was first through the unusual decision of Valentine to send the letters to a social research organisation shortly after she received them, and then, through the work of an archivist, Dorothy Sheridan, a historian, Penny Summerfield, a television researcher, and finally myself, in tracing and interviewing the surviving writers. In addition, conversations and correspondences between myself and the surviving letter writers, including Valentine, have added their own structures to the social scaffolding underneath this book. In the Epilogue, I explore how interpreting a set of archived letters has grown more complex as the writers themselves have offered their interpretations of what they wrote so long ago. Like the letters, such dialogues make their own versions of events not only out of memory but out of a relationship across class and between women. In considering these delicate compositions, I ask who is the author of the letter-book? Where is its authority?

But the partnership between editor, letter writer, collector and archivist is much more than a necessary compromise to make history out of letters. Rather, it is the origin of what is interesting about a letter collection in its own right. An improvised, patchwork history, a letter collection tells us about life as it is anticipated rather than remembered, shows us a relationship literally in the making. The letters in this book topple the icon of Rosie the Riveter by showing us the daily grind and struggle of women's experience of munitions work and wartime sexuality. The subsequent lives of the women who wrote them confirm this. But, when collected together as an unfolding narrative, they throw into relief other aspects of experience: the pleasure of friendship, of self-exploration and of writing. It is these facets of self-making that I have intended to bring out in publishing *Dear Laughing Motorbyke: Letters from Women Welders of the Second World War*.

I   Women Welders

Valentine's trainees did not choose to go into welding. They were drafted under the National Service (No. 2) Act, the 1941 law that conscripted women for the first time in British history.[4] They could be directed into welding, the services or some other 'vital war work', such as transport, Civil Defence, the Woman's Land Army, or nursing (Waller and Vaughan-Rees 1987: 61).

But if welding was not exactly a choice, it was not a huge change either. All of the women were working when they were drafted, and most of them were already in a factory. Munitions work had two big advantages. First, it allowed them to stay at home. This obviously avoided upheaval, and the dreaded discipline of service life. Amy recalled:

> I was called up when I was 28. Seeing that I was on air raid precautions I got that post for Hopkinsons, otherwise I would have had to go to Chorley into the powder factory . . . I didn't want to go away, Sheffield was just nice.[5]

The second good reason was money. Munitions workers were better off than those in the services and the women earned more than in their previous jobs. The four from Penistone had all been working as core-makers at David Brown's foundry, which employed about 60 women in that capacity. As the only four to move to welding, it was a novelty and a possible step up the ladder, filling the places of men who had been drafted.[6] The eight women from Huddersfield, when they were called up, were mainly employed in a local mill making fine worsteds, although Agnes had been a nanny and Enid was a seamstress. For them, too, welding certainly entailed no loss in status or work conditions. Yet Emily suggests that they may have wished for more:

> It were either that, you'd got to go in the army or this were the first thing that came up and . . . my mother wasn't very well at the time and I were near home, I was the last one at home you see, so that was that.[7]

Agnes's memory of being drafted into welding is ironic indeed, given the health hazards that the job involved:

I'd have liked to go into the air force. That was my first choice
. . . I had an ambition to be a telephonist because in those days I
spoke quite nicely, much more than I do now because I used to
take elocution lessons. Very posh. Anyway . . . I failed the medical.
So I had to go kind of where they sent me then and that was to
weld, to Welding Rods you see.[8]

In the disorganisation of the wartime economy the women were
given very little notice to leave their current jobs. It was 1942, the
middle year of the war, and the low point before the turn of the
Allies' fortunes. Britain was not to win its first land victory until
August, and the United States had only just entered the war. By then
rationing had been in force for two years, most of the men were
called up, the blitz and the blackout were a way of life. Helena
recalled that:

when we were going to work we were on shifts and it were pitch
black in the morning, you know there were no lamps or anything.
And I know we used to get up, we had to rush, not in the best
of tempers getting up at half past five in the morning.[9]

Dorothy adds:

I hated the atmosphere, the dark nights and no streetlamps and
everywhere blacked out and nobody had a cheerful fire 'cause they
hadn't enough coal. You couldn't get nice clothes with your
rationing . . . It wasn't a happy time . . . Well . . . we made the
most of it, we didn't sort of say oh it's miserable so we're going
to be miserable till the war ends. We used to go and have a good
time! but I wouldn't wish a war on anybody.[10]

But their time training at Welding Rods appears to have been the
high point not only of welding, but of their war. Being away from
home, with a chance to socialise, seems to have been heady. It wasn't
so much the welding as the freedom and the novelty, the fact that
the firm was small with a well-liked boss and a woman trainer.

The Penistone group commuted each day of their four-week
training. Helena remembered the silly jokes they played on the train
to Sheffield. Joan remembers having a sing-song. And Dorothy
comments: 'We did have fun. We were never back-biting were we?'[11]
She implied the same in her letter of 1942: 'Just a line to let you
know I am still living and have not forgotten how good you were

to us when we were at Welding Rods Lmt.' Despite the briefness
of their training, Helena reminisces: 'It were a drop coming back
to a foundry.'[12] And Dorothy writes to Valentine on starting
back at David Brown, 'Glad to hear the girls from Hopkinsons are
behaving themselves, but aren't they staying a long time – lucky
blighters' (Letter 5).

The 'girls from Hopkinsons' were the eight from Huddersfield.
Unlike the women from Penistone, they were not already working
at the foundry before they were called up, and they did not already
know each other. They stayed for six months, rather than the usual
training period of a month, because the factory was still being fitted
up for its new production of tanks and bridges. Valentine found them
billets in Sheffield, the most popular of which was with a policeman
and his wife, Mr and Mrs Holmes, and an extraordinarily fluent canary.
When they weren't welding, they went to the corner shop for
chocolate and biscuits, to the pub, to dances, and played jokes on
each other in the billet. Valentine's version is that:

> they didn't have any other friends there, except themselves, and
> . . . they were friendly together, but they all had little quirks about
> each other and, they'd make jokes, quite . . . sarcastic and hurtful
> jokes they'd say about each other, but they took it in good heart
> because basically they were very fond of each other, they had never
> met before. They were eight girls, suddenly thrown together and
> naturally they picked out each other's weaknesses and teased
> them about it . . .[13]

Emily, who appears from all accounts to have been a lively woman
of strong principles, describes herself as having being more interested
in welding than going out flirting or dancing. Throughout the war,
she waited for the return of her fiancé, who had been taken a
prisoner of war in 1940 in Germany. Ethel was courting John, an
engineer, whom she returned to see at the weekends in Huddersfield.
Nellie and Alice were slightly older than the others, in their late
twenties. Both of them were, as Valentine remembers them, quieter
and more sober than the others. Nellie was the only daughter of an
elderly and frail mother, whom she had cared for since her father's
death. Enid was an invisible mender and, according to both Valentine
and Ethel, very demure and neat.[14]

The two most prominent members of the group were Amy and
Agnes. Amy, according to Valentine, stood out in her tailored suits,
pork pie hat and brogues:

She was very forthright and she would tell people what to do. 'You ought to do so-and-so', you know, for their own good! She was shortish, a little solid person. She wore rather thick glasses, she had a pleasing face and a very nice smile and . . . she wasn't a butch or anything like that but she was dressing in that direction. And oh she had rosy cheeks, she looked almost like a country girl . . . She dressed in that style with nothing fripperty about her, lacy gloves or things, and she was very cheerful and she was frank and absolutely honest. I mean she'd give you an honest opinion.[15]

Amy is similarly remembered by her colleagues, as being fun-loving, unpretentious and 'uninterested in men'. Her niece, Stephanie Buckley, described her thus:

Mother always said she was the black sheep of the family. She talked to the family that they were forbidden to talk to. She fell in a pigpen and got impetigo. My grandparents never asked her to do anything in the house because she did it so badly. She never did what she was told. She was independent. She would go out drinking ales with Uncle Bill – just like me.[16]

One of Enid's letters gives a memorable snapshot of Amy at work at Hopkinsons:

Amy is still as lively as ever and runs round in circles trying to get her work done quickly. The other day Mr Robinson passed her cubicle and he said he thought there must be a dozen people in at least, and on looking found there was only our little 'Aimeeee' swearing away and carrying on 'something shocking' and just imagine Amy's horror when she heard later in the day that Mr R was a parson's son. (Letter 53)

Valentine declares that Amy:

arrived as being friendly with Emily. And then Agnes came and Agnes was such a colourful character that Amy was sort of fascinated by her and tagged along and Emily didn't particularly approve of this because Emily is very very conservative and she thought Agnes was at worst outrageous and at best somebody not to be too close to in case she got upset or . . . outraged.[17]

Agnes arrived to start training at Welding Rods a couple of
months after the other Huddersfield women had begun. Valentine
remembers her colour and zest:

> Agnes was flamboyant. And she . . . had a terrific sense of humour,
> it kind of boiled over. And she would recite . . . bawdy poems.
> Really bawdy, that shocked some of the girls. Especially Emily
> and Enid. Amy didn't mind. Amy egged her on . . . she'd come
> out with one of these dreadful poems that had most of us in hysterics
> and a couple of us in disapproving looks. And she . . . was . . .
> absolutely spontaneous. And of course when she arrived, she had
> just had her front teeth removed and she arrived with her new
> bridegroom and they were panting as they came because they were
> late you know. They arrived in a flurry of excitement and
> apparently her husband, who had joined the navy and arrived in
> his sailor boy uniform, was only 19. I didn't realise that. And he
> was on leave. So he fitted in very well. And the girls all liked him.
> And he was . . . unostentatious, he kind of kept out of the way,
> he didn't intrude. And he'd come to work and then he'd go off
> on his own, go to the pub or something and turn up for lunch.
> And he wasn't in the way at all. He was a very nice person. Actually
> Agnes really took advantage of him. So kind, and she sent him
> about doing all sorts of things, and she stood about keeping him
> waiting . . . She brought life into the room when she came in
> and she had ideas about all sorts of things, about serious things,
> and comical things, suppose she's what you call a livewire. And
> she was . . . painfully thin and she'd had all sorts of illnesses, terrible
> things . . . like being in bed for six weeks because of her [back]
> but . . . she'd come through them all.[18]

Agnes loved welding and quickly became proficient, despite her late
start. It was she who initiated a trip across town to Welding Rods'
laboratory to see how their practice welds on 'tubes' were tested by
being stretched and twisted, and, in her seventies, she was still
extremely proud to be able to say that she came out with top marks
for both theory and practice. Thin and tall, she earned the nickname
'Fanny Four Rod' after the size four welding rods that they used.
However, her fragile health and extreme thinness meant that she
was continually prey to illness and her employment at Hopkinsons,
although she stayed on until the end of the war, was chequered by
sick leave.

As for Valentine, she was a 'bit of a blue-stocking', according to Dorothy. Agnes, who knew her better, described her as a 'real rapscallion'.[19] The only daughter of conventional upper-middle-class parents, she was always seeking out adventurous encounters. 'She did things for the nerve of it,' Agnes adds, recalling her dressing in men's clothes and pushing her father in a lake for a bet. Valentine's diary account of the outbreak of the war gives us an idea of her sense of humour:

Sunday September 3, 1939

Arrived home 8.30, had bath and breakfast, did some cooking. 11.15 listened to PM's speech. Father spent morning enlarging pit in garage for shelter. Hastily blacked out windows of same pit with sacking. As a result of A.R.P. posters I expected a more or less constant shower of bombs from the moment war was declared, so had lunch early before it started. Argument at meal about German wine, which finished by 'When that's done I'm not getting any more' from Father. Several people phoned including cousin, 19, just returned early from holiday to empty house, so told him to come for night. Arrived 3, without gasmask, so sent back by mother to fetch same. Set him on to enlarging shelter. 8.30 aunt rang up demanding son to be sent home to black her out, she'd just arrived back from Whitley Bay by taxi, therefore outcry from family, including son, who delivered his personally over phone, at fresh example of extravagance (above aunt being family byword). Went to bed 9.30, after listening to News and Polish ambassador; as had to be up at 3 a.m. 3.30, woke from air raid warning, having slept through alarm clock, rushed down to pit, but returned to help family in search for gasmasks, bedroom slippers etc.; couldn't turn lights on as were not blacked out. All settled in pit, found cat missing, so set off on search for same and also returned to house for shoes and coat. Settled once more, Father next decided to go onto lawn to see if anything was going on, coaxed him back and pulled car over top of pit for additional safety. Next Father got bored so returned to house to make some tea. 4 a.m. all clear went; tore off to dress and arrived depot 4.25, it being very light night and easy to drive. Talked most of night in common room, slept on stretcher between 5 and 7 o'clock news.[20]

The diary also recounts volunteering to help local refugees in order to meet men, all the locals having been drafted. She was successful, finding a Czechoslovakian refugee Gottfried Morche, whom she married in 1943. During the period of the letters, she travelled most weekends to visit him at his different camp bases, where he was posted with the Czech regiment, outwitting the guards of protected areas by disguising herself as a local wife with rights of entry, her clothes hidden in a food basket.

Unlike her trainees, she had chosen to go into welding, albeit as a fall-back when her work as a graphic advertisement designer dried up in the approach to war. Her father, Mr Pearson, was the Managing Director of Welding Rods in Sheffield and:

> one Sunday afternoon I went down to my father's works and he said try your hand at welding, so I tried and it seemed quite easy and nice. So he said, well, why don't you get a job here and that's what I did and I was employed in . . . the department for making electrodes . . . experimenting with different slags.[21]

She was also sent to evening classes at the local university for two years to study metallurgy and eventually learned electric arc welding. But she found this far less interesting than when she began to teach, as the need for munitions workers grew. She proudly recalls her father's surprise on hearing her reputation at one firm where she worked as the 'young woman teacher with long, red nails'!

Was the fact that she was a young and irreverent woman, 27, the same age or younger than most of her trainees, also still at home with her parents, part of the reason that her women trainees decided to pick up the pen and write to her after finishing their training course? At any rate, she was delighted to reply. When work was dull she would leave the shop floor and compose on the office stationery, when she wasn't reconstituting lipsticks by melting their ends together over a welding torch.

The Penistone group were due to start their new jobs in February 1942. But the factory wasn't quite ready for them and they were put back on their old jobs of core-making ('making mud-pies' as Dorothy says disparagingly). The frustration that they felt is one of the central themes of the letters. Helena wrote of the new ambitions they had as 'girl welders':

> I suppose you'll have heard about the lovely big wages we're getting now, the times we've been in the offices since Christmas I wouldn't care to count, and after all our efforts, we get a 5/- rise, I wish they would rise me out of the firm for good. I drew for a

weeks wage £1-16-0 last week of coarse stoppages off, but how
do they expect a girl to live on that a week, after my board is paid
I've hardly enough to keep me in cigs, I wish we could get a job
in Sheffield, welding of coarse where there would be more money
and more work, as we have hardly anything to do, last week [Violet]
and I were working the 2–10 shift and after 5 o'clock we had to
do core-making, so you can tell how busy we are welding. If you
could tell us, Miss Pearson, of any firms in Sheffield wanting girl
welders we would see what could be done about us being released
from this dump of David Brown's, we are all fond of our job of
welding, and I, for one wouldn't like to give it up. (Letter 1)[22]

The women from Huddersfield had enjoyed a six-month-long
training precisely because their factory Hopkinsons had delayed
their employment until it was tooled up for war production. But
when they arrived in July they too discovered that the plant was far
from ready. Jenny writes:

there is one booth up and do they look funny. The machine hasn't
been coupled up yet or I should ask them if I could practise a bit
as I haven't got a job. I didn't know it was such hard work doing
nothing. (Letter 52)

And: 'We had quite a shock this week, we were told we may be
welding by Monday but alas and alack it is the usual nazi-report.'
Instead of welding, they were given gas cutting,[23] painting or sorting
pieces, or even doing nothing – which bored them to tears. Agnes
lets loose:

I have never been so disgusted in my life, at the disgraceful way
Hopkinsons Ltd, is managed. We are not welding, we are pushed
from pillar to post, and today, after asking the foreman for a job,
he said, 'Just stand there in that corner'. That was at 7-45 at the
latest, and at 3-15 in the afternoon, I was still standing in my corner.
In desperation, I walked over to where Ethel, and Jenny, were
painting, I very unconcerned sat down, and started, when who
should come pompously down, but Grandmother Marflitt. 'What
are you doing there?' said she, 'who gave you permission to sit
there?' I very steadily looked at her and said, 'I gave it to myself.'
I then told her I had been standing in a corner all day, and she
promised to speak to Willie Brooks. Nevertheless, neither of
them came, and I went there too, today, and nothing was said.

They are still setting girls on, and there is insufficient work for the ones already employed. I'm afraid if the truth was known about the actual facts, of the slackness of the workers, and the incompetence of its bosses – there would be trouble. We can smoke all day, and talk all day to our workers – even leaving our machines to do it, and nothing is said. I feel like saying a lot, I can tell you, and had I known a week ago what I know now, wild elephants would not have fetched me home from Scotland, war effort, or no war effort. (Letter 10)

The continually patronising attitudes of the foreman Willie Brooks and 'Grandmother Marflit', a shop-floor supervisor, are another theme of the letters. There seemed to be a similar character at David Brown's core shop, 'a real straight laced spinster', according to Helena. Perhaps they did not like the new confidence and status of the 'women welders', and they suggest what Penny Summerfield describes as the persistent tensions within as well as between classes, notwithstanding the celebrated social levelling of the People's War (Summerfield and Braybon 1987: 197–9). Agnes's letter provides an eloquent picture of the reality of the 'war effort', as it struggled through not only the technicalities of shortages and confused government policy but social miscommunications.

When the women finally did start welding, it was evidently a relief. At Brown's the women repaired the castings for tank parts and ship valves. At Hopkinsons, they did more skilled construction work, welding parts for bridges and tank vents. Valentine had taught them electric arc welding, which involved strength, great concentration and resistance to the heat, as well as a precise and steady hand.[24] One hand was used as a brace (or to hold a mask if they were not wearing one); the other hand held a 'welding rod' or electrode, in a clamp, which was attached to an electric generator. The rod was then struck against the pieces of metal to be welded, creating an electric circuit, the 'arc'. This heated the piece to fusion temperature, and the rod was melted down. The rod was coated with a powder that burned off, creating 'slag' on the weld to protect it from oxidisation. Valentine says that Agnes was an excellent welder because she had had practice decorating cakes, while Enid was helped by her skills as an invisible mender. A tricky aspect of the job was getting the distance and angle between the welding rod and the metal right. They had to maintain the rod about half a centimetre away. Too far away, and the electric arc would be extinguished, or the temperature would get too high and make a 'slag-hole'. Too near, and it would stick, mixing the slag into the metal, which would later have to be milled off. The timing also had to be precise. Too quick, the welding rod would simply melt without fusing it with the piece; too slow, it would create a blobby mess. Amy crows happily in one letter:

> One of the Welders at Hops put a Weld on our new device and what a slag-hole. I said 'My word if Mr Pearson saw us do a Weld like that we should be sacked!' (Letter 22)

Of course, such work was dirty and potentially dangerous. Indeed, one woman originally with the Huddersfield group hated it so much that she left the training almost immediately. (It was she who was replaced by Agnes.) Furthermore, when Jenny was sacked from Hopkinsons for 'being rude' to the manager, the others felt that it was what she'd been aiming for. They wore overalls, spats, leather aprons, asbestos gloves, goggles (to protect them from the slag), masks (hand-held) and slacks. An asbestos curtain surrounded the cubicles in which they worked. Amy writes to Valentine, 'I shall have to close now because I have that Brown Boiler Suit to patch before I go out' (Letter 33). The potential authority that women's new uniforms signified, both in industry and the services, is suggested by their treatment in contemporary advertising. Tampax, for example, displayed images of women making tanks, working at lathes and 'manning' anti-aircraft guns with a logo showing a woman in crinoline and bonnet, captioned 'Women are winning the War – of Freedom'. Yet such imagery was offset by advice to 'feminise' the uniform, or to perceive it as a merely superficial 'masculine' armour, necessary for the war effort. While Tampax claimed to liberate women from their 'natural disabilities', the corset makers Berlei showed a lathe operator in work clothes, next to a ghostly outline of the same woman wearing only a Berlei corset with the text:

> Her war service is helped by a secret service – the smooth, firm, supporting control of a Berlei. If you have to stand for long hours a Berlei, cut to *your* figure type, will correct your posture, lessen fatigue, give figure and clothes a lovely line . . . And a Berlei controlette, remember, needs only four coupons! (Waller and Vaughan-Rees 1987: 107)

The women did not bother with a 'controlette', but Amy writes of the 'performance' that the boiler suit caused:

Yes my dear we have got a new bib and brace overall each, except Alice. We have such a performance when we go to the corner, having to take the boiler suit off we thought we would have a change so we all step in, in new Battle dress tomorrow. (Letter 35)

Furthermore, Valentine considers that the women got burnt more often than the men because their protective clothing was thinner:

Men didn't get burnt because they had army uniforms, thick sleeves, long trousers and boots for uniform. Women's protective clothing was thinner. Women chose to dress in non-protective clothing. [They got] burns on their feet because [they] wore ordinary shoes and no stockings because [they] didn't want to burn them. Later on in the war they started wearing pants. [They] did have overalls. Girls got flashes partly because they weren't used to the work, and didn't realise the danger. Men also wore masks that fitted on to their heads – they didn't mind upsetting their hair. Masks made red marks around their forehead and upset your perm. Women therefore had handheld masks.[25]

Valentine too preferred style to safety at times. 'I didn't like the feel of a helmet (being enclosed) apart from the hair problem – though you would have to have that if you were doing a lot of overhead welding – pipe lines and so on.' She also didn't wear thick clothing – but she was only demonstrating so she didn't get burnt as often.

They were continually burnt by flying bits of slag, which could land in their ears while they chipped it off from a weld. The other most common problem was arc eye, caused by accidentally looking at 'flashes' of the intense light of the flame. Agnes said, 'You feel as if your eyes are full of sand',[26] and Valentine describes this as 'like soap in your eyes all night'.[27] Enid writes:

When Mr Pearson was round the other day, one of us must have given Mr Wright a flash and he came in with both his eyes bunged up the next day. He came straight down to the shop and had some more curtains fixed over the spaces of others so perhaps he knows what it feels like now. (Letter 53)

Amy also mentions:

We have all been knocked up with the heat today so there is going to be another row before long I will let you have details in my

next letter. Emily has burnt her face with slag so the nurse has
plastered it up also your pal Aimee is suffering once again with
half my face red and the other half white with the damned masks.
(Letter 34)

Valentine describes how at Stanton Iron Works, in Ilkeston,
Yorkshire, the women were asked to start work without protective
screens set up and:

> everybody got arc eye, including me thank goodness. So without
> much sleep we all arrived at work next morning, red eyed – their
> nearest and dearest were very upset and there was talk of them
> getting TB or blind. But to their credit they stayed on – they were
> as unique and interesting as the Huddersfield girls and we all had
> fun . . . The morning after the first arc-eye episode the management
> sent us all to walk round the local meadows – green being a healing
> colour! . . . We bathed our eyes with milk or tea (tannic acid)
> which helped a bit.[28]

There were no dust suctions for dust and fumes 'in those days',
says Valentine, and of course, all the protective materials were made
from asbestos. Dorothy at Brown's was left with a legacy of continual
laryngitis, and Joan describes how the continual noise of 'steel on
steel' has permanently damaged her hearing.[29] Agnes describes how
her performances with the Hopkinsons' Operatic Society had to be
entirely rewritten as the fumes had changed her soprano into a tenor:

> I did enjoy the job. But it didn't enjoy me . . . I was in the operatic
> society at Hopkinsons and I used to be able to trill up on top Cs
> and top As . . . and I suddenly felt in rehearsal I wasn't getting
> them with the ease that I used to do and I gradually dropped and
> dropped and dropped and dropped till I was croaking like a frog
> right down in the basement. And that's when they fetched me
> out and they drew me out because the fumes were getting . . . to
> me chest.[30]

Both David Brown and Hopkinsons had medical facilities staffed by
full-time nurses, who were remembered as very good. But none of
the women were ever compensated for the effects on their health.

If some of these health hazards may have been the effect of
women's inexperience or conditioning, the overall problem was that
any complaint could be interpreted as evidence that women were

fundamentally unsuited for the job. Clearly, if the women had attempted to claim compensation or extra protection, they were likely to have been diverted into the debate over whether women should be allowed to do such work in the first place. The no-win position that this put them in is most obvious in an incident when the Hopkinsons' team found they were having menstrual problems that they thought might have been due to the heat. Emily's account of this shows clearly that for her this was evidence not only of the bad conditions of work, but its inappropriate nature for women:

> We were stood over them things for eight hours a day. Red hot things. And every one of us had excessive periods. Now if it isn't the job, what is it? There's not eight girls having excessive periods for no reason at all is there? So I got on to Sister Ripley about this. She said, 'Well we'll take it further. We'll go to the medical officer involved,' and [they had Valentine Pearson come down to interview us] as I remember it rightly, if I've got my facts right. And she said, 'No way could welding cause it.' She wasn't doing the amount of welding we were doing so I don't think she realised the amount of welding we were doing. Now Agnes's baby and my baby, we both had trouble, same trouble. [I had a] . . . calcified ovary down this side where you're getting all the heat and her baby was the same and she were born with a stiff neck like that and John were born just the same and we both went to hospital at the same time for treatment . . . But no thanks to them down there . . . because [Valentine] wouldn't stand up for us. Well Sister Ripley did her best but I think we could have got out earlier. Because it isn't a woman's job when all's said and done.[31]

The account also shows the tension between Valentine and the women, where she was perceived to have gone over to the bosses' side. At the same time Valentine's stand suggests that her minimising the effect on women's periods was motivated by her wish to defend a woman's right to do the job – although perhaps at the cost of a real appreciation of its difficult conditions.[32]

'For the duration'

These contradictions reflected a much larger dilemma in government policies over the use of women's labour in heavy industry or other traditionally 'male' domains. The need for women was balanced by the government's wish to maintain the social order, a wish, indeed, strengthened in the upheaval of war. This meant that the new forms of women's employment were always seen as 'for the duration' only, an emergency measure whose aim was to keep the war machine going rather than to change the sexual division of labour. It was assumed that after the war they would return to their primary occupations of wife and mother. As Cynthia Enloe explains, this meant that all the major Axis and Allied governments

> tried to justify the recruitment of women workers without upsetting existing gender ideology and the sexual division of labour . . . Connie Field's film *The Life and Times of Rosie the Riveter* includes clips from 1940s American government films aimed at the 'mobile woman'. Women – all of them white – are shown using electric tools to make holes in aircraft wings, as the narrator reassures the audience, 'this is just like punching holes in your scouring powder tin'. And, for women, welding fighter planes was 'just like sewing'. (Enloe 1988: 178, 184)

In Britain too women were 'encouraged . . . to relate to their new jobs in ways that reinforced, not challenged, their presumed pre-war family dependencies and obligations' (184). The government initially exempted married women or women with children or other dependants from conscription, under what was known as the Household Responsibility Rule. To recruit them would have meant challenging the notion that child care, cleaning, shopping and the like were women's private responsibilities. Of course, many women wanted to do the child care, or keep control over what was their traditional domain, and welcomed the 'Household R' rule. (Notably, however, Nellie, who looked after her elderly mother, did not appear to have tried to escape conscription this way, nor did Agnes and Joan, who were married to servicemen.) The point, however, was unprecedented public acknowledgement that domestic work could be socialised and paid for. To some degree, this is precisely what happened. For as the war dragged on, the Ministry of Labour increasingly realised that it could not avoid employing women with domestic responsibilities.

Eventually, the government had to give in. By 1943, 43 per cent of women in paid work were married. This was a dramatic leap from 16 per cent in 1931, and a U-turn from the policy of barring married women that most professions still held to in the 1930s (Summerfield 1984: 31).[33] It was in response to the 'inefficiencies' and 'irregularities' of these workers that the famous schemes of state nurseries and 'British

Restaurants',[34] and, in part, rationing itself, were developed. But they were all far less embracing than has been subsequently thought. Despite the image of the war as a time when 'nurseries and crèches sprang up overnight' (Phillips 1987: 21), at the height of child-care provision, a 1944 survey showed that 50 per cent of married women workers complained about the difficulty of coping with domestic tasks because of their work (Hunt 1988: 10). At that time, places were available for 'at the most 25 per cent of the under-five-year-old children of women war workers', and that the same year three-quarters of the children of women war workers were cared for by minders, the traditional means of child care (Summerfield 1984: 84). Similarly, the schemes designed to help with cooking and shopping were limited; instead, employers preferred to give women long lunch hours or unpaid leave in order to fit in their 'double burden'. As Penny Summerfield has theorised, much of this was merely a regularisation of the way that working women had coped before the war.

Neither Hopkinsons nor David Brown provided crèche facilities or shopping aids, although they did have canteens. This may have been because most of their women workers were young and without children. But what would women workers have done if they had had children while at Hopkinsons? It is significant that one of the writers succeeded in her wish to terminate a pregnancy, and that Amy writes elliptically of a 'birth in the Lav'. Furthermore, although most of them didn't suffer from a double burden as mothers, they certainly did as daughters, and it was more than likely that they had to turn over most of their wages to parents.

There were, of course, some committed and visionary policy-makers and feminists, such as Edith Summerskill, Irene Ward and Lady Astor, members of a cross-party parliamentary caucus titled the Women Power Committee, who saw the exigencies of the war as an opportunity for long-term social change.[35] But they were checked by the majority of policy-makers, who wanted to preserve the social order at all costs.[36] The same pattern could be seen in the way that other opportunities for social levelling were contained. The need for labour had also helped those from ethnic minorities, the Irish, and the disabled into better-paid employment, but they too were disappointed at the end of the war as they were laid off to make room for the 'returning heroes'.

Women were therefore never really integrated into the kind of 'male' jobs and positions that they took up 'for the duration'. Instead, work such as welding was 'feminised', in a reconfiguration of the

Ruby Loftus screwing a breech-ring (oil on canvas) Dame Laura Knight, undated.
Imperial War Museum, London (LD 2850)

This relatively 'light' electric welding was close to what the
women did much of the time, particularly at David Brown.
Imperial War Museum, London (FX 3912C)

29, SHE'S THE SCHOOL MARM' TO RAF WELDERS IN GIANT CLASSROOM

Miss Pearson with some of her pupils, teaching them to do electric welding. See story in next column.

In a huge steel chamber, inside a Sheffield factory, RAF trainees learn the art of welding from their " school marm "—29-year-old dark-haired, dainty Sheffield miss.

They know their teacher as Miss Valentine Pearson, but in private life she is Mrs. Gottfried Fritsche, wife of a Czechoslovak soldier.

Miss Pearson disavows that welding is dirty, for she wears dainty frocks and manages to keep her hands clean and well manicured amidst the splutters and fiery glares of her giant classroom.

" If I go to my husband's country after the war, I hope to keep on with welding, as there will be great scope there," she told the Daily Mirror.

Valentine Pearson's teaching hits the national press.
Daily Mirror, early 1940s

Valentine Pearson and Gottfried Morche, circa 1942

Amy Brooke (left) and Agnes Helme, circa 1942

Gas cutting. The women at Hopkinson's had to do much of this before
their welding machines were ready.
Imperial War Museum, London (TP 4093D)

The different protective uniforms show an
electric arc welder (left) and an oxyacetylene
welder (right). Note the wedding rings.
Imperial War Museum, London (FX 14812C)

sexual division of labour. This was achieved in three ways. First, as we have seen, propaganda encouraged women to see their war work in terms of an extension of their domestic skills. Second, factory managers often redesigned entire processes so that they could 'incorporate women with as little investment in their training as possible'. Enloe points out that in this way the war simply accelerated long-term processes of mechanisation and de-skilling in factory work (184), but often this was intertwined with ideologies about 'women's special capacities' to do repetitive, monotonous yet accurate and delicate manual work. Third, and this was in part the reason for such restructuring, 'feminisation' meant that women were paid less. It is in this 'feminised' version that women's participation in industrial and military manufacture was made permanent. Today's military industries still use women workers across the globe to fill unskilled, low-paid or dangerous jobs in the manufacture of electronic weaponry, and they justify the 'special' advantages of these workers in much the same terms.[37]

It is therefore unsurprising that the women who wrote these letters were given what was only a basic, 'emergency' training in welding. Even the 'Welding Wonders' from Huddersfield, with their unusually long training, were only taught to weld in one position (horizontally rather than vertically or overhead). In contrast, Valentine taught a fully professional range of skills to her male trainees, whom she said in any case were often men who had worked in the metal industry before call-up. Her own professional training, as we have seen, was in the context of effectively working for her father. She recalls:

> the girls just had to learn how to make one particular thing . . . the whole of the war, they just welded this one special thing, or sometimes it might be changed to something else. They didn't have to use their ingenuity – they weren't doing repair work, they were just doing construction work . . . of course they could have [done repair work], if they were efficient enough to adapt to something if . . . somebody handed them something to do. It's like if you work in a garment factory, you perhaps would make only one thing, only make sleeves, only make collars . . . But if you could do that, you could probably make a collar or you could make a sleeve, or you could make a whole blouse.

As Valentine points out, despite the limitations of what the women were taught, they could certainly have been good enough to develop broader capacities. Indeed, at Hopkinsons none of the men initially knew the work as well as the women and Emily was asked to train several men up herself. But, the women were also paid less than their male colleagues. Helena says that they got about £4 a week, which was 'a good wage actually'. This was about 9 shillings more than they had been paid as core-makers. For comparison, the pre-war average wage was £1 10s a week; average earnings in 1944 reached £3 and a private soldier's wife with two children only received £1 13s in 1940 (Summerfield and Braybon 1987: 185). Yet this was 'nowhere near' what men were paid.[38] Dorothy Adams confirms this, saying that they never received more than half of what the men did, and that right at the beginning they got less than when they were core-making:

> JB: They couldn't give us [the] same as men got, that's what the excuse was.
> DA: Because they were jealous, they didn't want us to be as good as them.

At Hopkinsons, the women earned around £5 a week, for their long hours, and they had to argue to get that.[39] Emily explains that she engineered a pay rise through prompting the management to undertake a time and motion study to establish them on piece work. She describes how 'with a bit of twisting and turning' she exaggerated the time it took them to do a bracket from half an hour to an hour and three-quarters.[40] This way, the women could work more quickly and claim a bonus. Interestingly, the two male welders who also worked in their section were given the same rates. But clearly a higher monthly or daily wage would have signified a more permanent recognition of their work.

Did the unions take up the cause of women workers? Penny Summerfield, who has studied union history from the period, concludes that men were more likely to fear being undercut by women's 'cheaper' labour, and to feel a threat to their manhood than to make common cause with other exploited workers. After much lobbying, the Amalgamated Engineering Union, which organised welders, first accepted women in 1943, and then only with many qualifications that prevented women from having their work classified as skilled, or gaining male rates of pay. Amy writes, 'We have heard that the men are playing hell over the women welders, so it looks like more trouble for us' (Letter 26) and Valentine remembers being called in by one factory to persuade a trade unionist to train the women placements:

> he was forbidden by his union to do it and that's why I was sent there, because I was a woman . . . both men belonged to unions and I didn't . . . and the union couldn't go on strike over me. But I explained to him that they were only doing it for this time, they were dying to get back to their homes, whether it was true or not. He accepted that . . . I mean there was almost a riot going on at this place . . . The other men were all siding with the men. 'We don't want women!' There was somewhere else they didn't want women to come – I think it was Hopkinsons – at first. The men wouldn't speak to the women. And . . . to calm this man down here, the spokesman, I said to him it was nothing to worry about because when the war was over the women would go back home.[41]

It may be for this reason that the women at Hopkinsons didn't join the union at all. Emily remembers refusing to join a strike, saying that it wasn't right in wartime. But refusing to strike may also have indicated how little the women identified with the long-term structures of the workplace. While there is an intriguing reference to a strike in one of Amy's letters, what stands out is her neglect to say why they were striking. What seems important to her instead is whether her behaviour there jeopardised her femininity:

> I am being true to Chick now for a short while because if he keeps hearing tales about the Welders of Hopkinsons he will always be getting hurt. I met him yesterday afternoon for an hour before I met Emily. Yes he has come round, trust me to bring him too. He heard the men saying we had a sit down strike, and that the girl with glasses on, pink ones, said bugar it I am going home, so he was upset to think I had been swearing anyhow I told him it was a lie and he said he was glad it was, because he did not want me to start cursing like men, goodness knows it was bad enough for him, me working amongst them, without talking like them, however all is well now and I meet him again next Friday. Honest if he knew how much I did swear he would go mad, but I will watch he does not hear anymore about me I will see if I cannot control my feelings a bit in future. (Letter 35)

At David Brown, the women's scepticism about the union was a
very simple matter, for there the representative actually persuaded
the boss not to give the women equal pay. Dorothy remembers, 'We'd
have got more if he'd have kept his mouth shut. But he wouldn't
let us have it. It wasn't [that the] boss didn't want us to have it. *He*
didn't want us to have it.'[42]

Finally, although the women from both Brown's and Hopkinsons
remember their male colleagues being friendly, fun and helpful,[43]
there are glimpses in the letters that the constant banter between
the sexes could be double-edged. Jenny writes, 'We have a terrible
time with the fellows they tease us awful. Enid has a new name now.
Daphne Squeaker, because they say she squeaks when she gets mad
. . . Everything is so dull at work . . .' (Letter 52). Amy, who was
sent back to Hopkinsons with Emily three weeks earlier than the
other girls to prepare the plant, was dismayed that she was to be
separated from Emily as well:

> I am very upset about being alone amongst all the men but I shall
> have to face it I expect, it would not be so bad if there were some
> more girls in the room. (Letter 22)

Of David Brown, Helena comments, 'if you'd a good foreman you
were all right'. But she remembers that

> The charge hand over us . . . now he used to sneak into your
> welding booth you know and touch your bum. Of course you
> jumped . . . if you were welding, and of course you daren't say
> a right lot . . . but I mean you really had to put your foot down
> . . . It were alright with trousers on. We used to say 'Get out' . . .
> But I mean [he was a] charge hand, you couldn't stop him going
> in you see.[44]

Feminism and the war

We have seen that in many ways, the apparent 'revolution' in
women's roles was very superficial. While the entry of married
women into the labour market was more or less permanent,
Summerfield concludes that:

> If the experience of mobilising women for war shifted the
> assumptions and ideologies of policy-makers and employers about

women and work at all, it was in the direction of the idea that women could combine paid and domestic work without damage to industrial productivity and without undermining the concept that their first responsibility was to their homes. (Summerfield 1984: 188)

Yet one permanent legacy of the war is precisely the way it so usefully spotlit the sexual division of labour. Indeed, in this respect, it is something of a test case for different theories of what maintains women's – and men's – different roles and oppressions. The American feminist, Susan B. Anthony II, was one who tried to think through the underlying logic of those positions at the time.[45] In her cleverly argued polemic of 1943, *Out of the Kitchen, Into the War: Women's Winning Role in the Nation's Drama*, she interpreted the war in the United States as an (albeit ironic) opportunity not only for women, but for all those marginalised and disempowered, such as blacks, the elderly and the disabled (Anthony 1943: 65). Underlying her polemic was an analysis of women's oppression as economic. Liberation, in her view, therefore depended not only on women gaining access to the public sphere, but the state taking responsibility for the private:

> What we can learn from the British . . . is that no amount of compulsion – just as no amount of high pressure advertising – is effective to recruit women for war jobs unless, concurrently, the government manages to relieve women of housekeeping as usual. (66–7)[46]

Women's failure to make permanent gains in the structure of male employment was, from this perspective, linked to the elitism of feminism up till then dominated by 'disgruntled rich women'. In no uncertain terms, she argued that women's low status is 'not because men willed it . . . but because of the inherent nature of the ownership of property' (31). Real changes in women's position depended upon making common cause with the majority of women burdened by poverty as much as prejudice or abuse (32).

Anthony's thesis is supported by the fact that for upper-class women, the war *did* provide a more permanent opportunity to get into law, medicine or government, in contrast to the treatment of working-class women. It also points up the limits of the theory that the war broke down class divisions. Summerfield says that:

> The evidence supports the idea of social segregation rather than the real mixing of classes. It is hard to find figures showing the

social class of wartime factory workers, but surveys show that the vast majority had been in elementary school only, and a better-educated middle-class woman was an unusual and much-noticed phenomenon on the factory floor . . . At the same time, the war does stand out in many women's memories as a time when they mixed with people whom they would never normally have met. (Summerfield and Braybon 1987: 197–8)

The encounter between Valentine and her women students certainly fits this description of an unexpected encounter without any real breakdown of class difference. While it was clearly interesting enough on both sides to produce two life-long friendships, the different paths that she and they took after the war suggest that their perspectives, as well as their material opportunities, remained far apart.

Anthony's solution of a feminism founded on material levelling is a powerful one. Yet it does not explain why labour should be divided by sex in the first place. The principle of sexual segregation, of course, lies at the very heart of military organisation and is one which saturates wartime culture. But it is one which oppresses not only women but men, even more starkly, perhaps, in war. The economic interest in using women as a 'reserve army of labour', in this light, is merely a rationale for an older conception of sexual role rooted in notions of the protecting male warrior and the protected, domestic wife or mother. Any explanation of how women experienced the war must take into account this ideology and highlight a demand for the transformation of sexual identity and role.

It is patriarchal rather than capitalist ideology which prevents the upsurge of feminism during wartime, which so obviously tests the sexual division of labour upon which war is organised. The strength of this sexual rather than economic ideology is what would seem to have prevented most women during the war from interpreting women's entry into the public sphere in terms of long-term claims for their independence, rather than patriotic sacrifice. Anthony is right to say that working-class women like welders probably never identified with feminism partly because their priorities were economic. But even a glance at the letters in this book shows that sexual expectations and structures were just as crucial to their oppression. Despite the fact that the war did liberalise social and sexual behaviour, for example in terms of pre-marital sex and divorce, these changes didn't really change attitudes towards that double standard.[47] This is perhaps the biggest testimony of the letters in this book.

Yet the patriarchal ideology of militarism is riddled with contradictions. Not only the conscription of women but the technological effect of aerial warfare in the Second World War revealed the notion of men protecting women as a myth. And as Cynthia Enloe has argued, the war economy and male military morale have depended upon women's labour for centuries:

> Rosie the Riveter and her sisters were not the first women defence workers. Every time a camp follower cooked a meal for soldiers in order to obtain meagre rations, every time a soldier's wife sewed a uniform in a government garment factory, a woman was contributing her labour to the war machine, and, in turn, was becoming economically dependent on that war machine. (Enloe 1988: 174)

Exposing the ideal of autonomous masculinity and dependent femininity for the exploitative fictions they really are, is one of the ways in which women's personal testimony, like the letters in this book, can be so useful. If we read the letters closely in this light, we see that the welders' representation of their identities is much more complex than the position of waiting women, doing their bit for 'our boys', allows. Their attempt to make sense of their lives within patriarchal ideology, and sometimes to challenge it, can expose its contradictions.

For, despite these frustrations, the women were proud of their work and enjoyed the new jobs and leisure. 'I always remember Mr Pearson saying, "Welding isn't a job, it's an art," ' commented Helena,[48] and Dorothy remembers that it was 'smashing at dances' where 'you used to meet lads from all over'. Joan adds that wartime was 'a happy time because everybody . . . were all right nice, you used to work, you used to have some fun and, out at war and everything, you weren't miserable'.[49] 'Work isn't going down too bad, and good to say I never get bored with welding,' she wrote at the time. Ethel too states that she 'loved welding', and Agnes now happily confesses that, at Hopkinsons, the women got away with murder:

> We had life and they daren't say anything to us because there was nobody could tell us what to do. We were allowed an hour and three quarters to do a bracket . . . Well . . . we could actually, if we really worked quickly, do a bracket in twenty minutes, which we didn't usually unless we were really exerting ourselves, usually

make it about half an hour and then for that other quarter you
see while they were putting us another bracket on, we went to
cool off and we went anywhere in the world and upset him . . .
One of the managing directors when he used to come past, they
used to start singing 'Down boys, underneath'. They only made
it to his step. Oh we died of laughter. They'll never forget the
welders at Hopkinsons. One April Fools' day we fastened a right
big coil of – you know when you turn on a lathe? . . . Well we
fastened a right long tail of that on one of the managing director's
smocks. He had it on for hours. And all the men were killing
themselves from laughing you know. Oh we were real monkeys.[50]

Of course, one of the most direct products of this enjoyment is
the letters themselves. The sheer irreverence and the spirit of the
writing as well as the connection with Valentine that they represent
is testimony to what could be made out of the war experience. For
the letters are as much creative writing as historical document. The
next section looks at them in literary terms, to argue that, by
appreciating letter writing as a popular art, we can also access some
of the women's individual interpretation of their circumstances.

II   The Popular Art of Letter-writing

For most of the women, their relationship with Valentine was only
temporary, and they wrote simply to say thank you and goodbye.
Yet what is striking is how even a limited, conditional acquaintance
engendered such creative writing. This simplest kind of writing pact,
the thank-you letter, is transformed by a language of romance,
jokes, puns and dialect that exceeds the literal. News and enquiry
are structured as tale or confession, displaying what Patricia Spacks
has analysed as characteristic of the creative dimension of gossip: an
'aesthetic of self-containment, concentration on surface, valorising
of story' (Spacks 1986: 16).

Attention to the language and perspective of the letters also reveals
the subtler dimensions of the relationship between Valentine and
her students. Both the ambiguous style, at once teasing and deferential,
and the recurring theme of (hetero)sexuality signal what were
potentially creative tensions in the relationship. On the one hand,
a wide difference in social status made friendship unlikely. But on
the other hand, the correspondence represents a sense of common
interest. This seems to spring from their shared identity as women

challenging the sexual double standard of wartime mores. Thus, while the letters are not 'literary' in any canonical sense, close reading shows that they were a space for inventiveness and autobiography of a sometimes unexpected kind. Indeed, it suggests that we need to broaden the limited terms of literary criticism, which not only marginalise letters as a genre but largely dismiss working-class correspondence as 'merely' a means of communication.

Bad girls/good correspondents

Every letter shares the paradox that, while its *raison d'être* is to bridge separated people, it must communicate by projection and construction. In the case of the welders' letters, this constructive nature of correspondence is particularly strong. This is, in part, simply because they did not know each other well and therefore could not write intimately. But it is also because they were clearly writing *about* their social difference. Familiarity jostles uneasily alongside formality, signalling Valentine's status as patron *and* confidante. Some of the letters refer self-consciously to the awkwardness of how to address her. Not wishing to use her first name, extravagant nicknames are adopted, sometimes tinged with sexual innuendo. Nellie moves from a polite 'Dear Miss Pearson' at the top of the letter to a laughing 'Madam Pearson' in a PS, where she has to bring up the subject of holiday pay, and does so in a pun that seems to have been a running joke in the group about 'having it' (Letter 48). More strikingly, shortly after addressing a letter 'Dear little glamour girl Hearthrob No 1', Amy writes:

> I must say one thing. I thank you very much for giving me permission to use your Christian name, but under circumstances I regret I could not, I would sooner give up writing to you altogether thank you all the same. (Letter 23)

The most baroque of all the addresses is this, from Agnes:

> My Dear Laughing Motorbyke,
>
> I hope you are having no trouble in aquiring your petrel ration, because should you have to garage your laugh, you would hardly be the same person, at least to me. (Letter 10)

This wonderful metaphor must have surely activated Valentine's engine-like laugh.[51] However, Agnes's declaration of friendship suggests how much the wish to charm Valentine involved social aspiration:

> I'm not in the habit of paying compliments, nor do I like receiving them, (in spite of my dumb expression, as you claim) but I don't think you can possibly conceive how much real pleasure and how honoured I feel, to have your friendship. Please don't think I'm offering you strawberries, and cream on a silver platter, or that I am paving the way to borrow something or other, I am merely stating a fact. (Letter 16)

Strawberries, cream and silver are spurned as flattery, but suggest the luxury Agnes finds in the friendship. The bold imagery goes beyond 'merely stating a fact', in creating, as well as reflecting, the relationship, but the terms of that creation are caught up in the inequalities of authority and status.

At the same time, the letters escape the usual pattern of correspondences between writers of different classes which are typically engendered by the notion of an improving or educating dialogue, in which the working-class correspondent 'writes up'. It is not that Valentine was overtly political or even interested in the question of class. She wasn't. Indeed, in interview she said, 'I was like a mother to them', despite the similarity in age, which suggests she never went as far as considering the exchange to be an equal one. If her letters had survived, although we can only speculate, we can imagine that she continued her 'teacherly' role, eliciting more than she tells. Yet, within this, it appears from the welders' letters that she encouraged self-imagining outside the strictures of respect, fidelity and obedience that surround them. She did also, it appears, circulate some stories of her own escapades, notably one of a night she slept under a hedge with her serviceman boyfriend, after they had been unable to pass themselves off as a married couple at a hotel. Several of the welders made jokes out of it, including addressing their letters to 'Dear Vagrant'.

The following letter from Nellie demonstrates some of the unorthodox writing that the correspondence produced. Recovering from illness, she writes to thank Valentine for some flowers:

Dear Miss Pearson.

Am writing in ink, but I am another step higher, sitting in the room now, and just walked down the street, felt grand.

Received your most charming letters, did me good I can tell you, I laughed at the sleeping out bit. We ought to be playing 'consequences' would have pulled your leg.

Do you know dear, I received the flowers on my Birthday, what a pleasant surprise, people that came to see me, said 'How lovely', smell, smell, till I thought there wont be any roses left and no smell.

Of course the 'twins' [Amy and Emily] had to take a flower, they have been everyday,[52] shall miss them next week, received letters from the girls, if Fanny [Agnes] does not go anywhere next week, will write and ask her to come, she does want to see me she says.

Sid's Mother [her boyfriend's mother] would like me to go when I feel stronger and have a few days, but shall not sleep under the hedge. (now then Nellie none of that) so now dear I must close, thanking you again for your kindness, and will write again to you, do remember me to the 'Miss A.T.S.' and will tell her very quickly, when I do the 'Big Thing'

With Best Wishes
yours Sincerely
Nellie.

P.S. Alice 'Old Faithful' [another of the welders] has just called, but to my dismay I thought I was receiving my 'Holiday with Pay', she laughed when she saw my face or shall I say 'Mug drop' when she hadn't it. What about Madam Pearson aren't I entitled to it or can't I 'HAVE IT'.

Something else now.

Cheerio. Nell. (Letter 48)

What is striking about this letter is its spontaneity – jumping out at you with that emphatic present tense of 'smell, smell'. Thanking Valentine for the flowers, she does not write as a passive recipient of bounty but amusingly parodies her visitors' mechanical reactions of admiration – 'How lovely' – surreally suggesting that just smelling them will exhaust them. Her description of Emily and Amy, the 'twins'' determination to take one of the flowers also suggests an edge of detachment, while neatly leading into news of Valentine's other old trainees.

The other striking thing about the letter is the sexual nature of the tease, most obvious in her 'joke' ending to Valentine's story of

sleeping out. This game of sexual 'Consequences' is clearly one that
Nellie perceives them both to be playing, even if only on the level
of wishing:

> Sid's Mother would like me to go when I feel stronger and have
> a few days, but shall not sleep under the hedge. (now then Nellie
> none of that) (Letter 48)

In the final aside, the ambiguity of whether she mustn't tease
Valentine or whether she mustn't sleep under hedges herself suggests
the way that the letters are fuelled by a mutual interest in being
'bad girls'.

Nellie's letters, with Agnes's and Amy's, are the most interesting
in these terms. But close reading of all the letters suggests that it is
this 'talking bad', or rather 'fun' that provides a common language
across the wide difference of class and professional status.[53] This is
in some ways ironic. They may have shared more experience at work
than at home, as women welders, but it is richly suggestive in terms
of how both Valentine and her trainees experienced their sexual
identity as more important than their class identity in this context.
Indeed, in this sense, the letters – and the relationship that they both
express and construct – support the argument that the war experience
was crucial to a reconceptualisation of femininity as actively sexual,
in which differences of class, culture or ethnicity, were often less
important than the bond of youth. This is perhaps most succinctly
expressed in a moment of Violet's one letter:

> Well Val I hope you don't mind me calling you that? but how is
> your boy friend getting on with Army life do you know we have
> been looking for a letter to say that you were getting Married but
> no fear I think you are like Helena and I you want a good time
> first. (Letter 8)

Violet drops her formal 'Miss Pearson' for the familiar 'Val' in order
to ask after Valentine's romance, underlining their common identity
as women of pleasure. But clearly, the 'good time' she boldly evokes
is explicitly expected to end with marriage.[54]

The emphasis on pleasure and 'naughtiness' therefore is always
double-edged, both denying and acknowledging the sexual struggles
that women wage in peacetime as much as in war. In this sense, they
form an interesting parallel to the kinds of popular culture of rumour,
joke and swearing that Paul Fussell has analysed in the world of male

wartime service. For Fussell, these forms both involve imaginative wit and a deep psychological need to make sense of the demeaning rules of much of military life as well as more obvious fears for survival:

> During wartime there seems less need for high narrative, like sophisticated romance or novel, than low. Folk-narrative (or officially generated pseudo-folk-narrative) blossoms on all sides. The most common form of folk-narrative is the dirty joke. It survives abundantly in wartime, but it is joined by such psychologically useful forms as the myth of military heroism and the compensatory rumor . . .
>
> Perhaps rumors should be taken more seriously by students of narrative. Certainly they seem to exhibit an analyzable taxonomy. If some are satires exposing the stupidity of one's own side or demeaning the enemy, others are virtual romances, rendering an optimistic and ideal vision of the future . . . 'Romance' or consolatory rumors . . . resemble horror rumors turned inside out. Instead of stimulating fear without facts, they propose hope without facts. (Fussell 1989: 35, 43)

Fussell implies that such creativity is rooted in desperation. Civilian women like these letter writers were neither restricted to camp life nor, in their case, in danger of their lives. Yet the 'dirty' jokes, swearing, poems and ironic rumours that circulate in the letters also reflect the forces that control and limit their lives. Courtship, pregnancy, abortion, sexual harassment, sexual desire, all appear as fodder for what is ambiguously both entertainment and confession. Agnes amuses Valentine with jokes of this order: 'A woman was being chased by a huge Bull. A man looking over the hedge shouted, "what are you running for lady, can't you take it?" "Of course I can take it, but I can't keep a calf in a council house"!!!' (Letter 10). Enid's account of her 'housekeeping practice' confesses to innocence:

> Cyril and I are going housekeeping tonight some friends of ours who haven't been married long keep lending us their key to get some practice, they say. The last time we went Frank and Phil came back and were surprised to find us playing Monopoly. I wonder what they expected. (Letter 53)

Amy typically goes much nearer the edge of such humour, instructing Valentine 'if you hear of any more births in the Lav – please study because you never know what will happen now my guide is leaving me' (Letter 21).[55]

The three letters from John Kergon (Ethel's fiancé) in the collection, thus offer a piquant contrast to these loaded jokes. Kergon, an engineer, wrote to Valentine (whom he never met) to help him win Ethel's hand. His opening letter approaches a Victorian formality at points, but adopts a chatty familiarity when he describes his relationship:

> I've taken the liberty of asking you a favour, perhaps to you it will look like a piece of unheard of cheek, I suppose it is, but I'd do anything for Ethel, to get to the point though, I wonder if you remember having a conversation with Ethel, about an engagement ring, one she had seen, I think there was a green centre to it, I gathered, by the talk, that she would have liked it very much, of course she did not say so, but I would like to give her a pleasant surprise, as well as a ring, I'm afraid I can only do this with your help . . . until I know then, I wish to remain, in anticipation of being forever in your debt,
> Yours faithfully
> John Kergon (Letter 41)

Kergon's letter of request is also a letter of confidence, yet there is an interesting dissonance between the language of confiding and that of slightly courtly entreaty. This suggests that Valentine's status as the providing boss overrides his as the providing man. This is even more pronounced in the second letter in which he immediately adopts the casual address of 'Dear Val', confesses that he is 'a bit scared' of giving Ethel the ring. The final letter confesses masculine vulnerability with humorous charm. Although 'everything went off as per plan and was Ethel pleased!' (Letter 43), he adds that 'I popped the ? in the pictures on Saturday night, and "boy" had I a sweat on! and had to mop my brow a bit at first, and after you had told me to be cool and collected too!, I forgot all that and everything else.' Valentine is again constructed as benevolently powerful, yet there is a different tone to the women's negotiation of the difference in status. An obvious point of contrast is his opening comment in the last letter that: 'Ethel headed this [the address] but thought Dear Val too familiar! and wouldn't go any further and so, well here I am.' His increasing colloquialism, with its self-conscious 'American' slang, both concedes and asserts the difference in status, as it deliberately flouts epistolary convention, here obviously to Ethel's distress. But if his style is less formal than the women's, it is also less ironic, as clearly he cannot appeal to a common 'dissidence' as bad girl and woman welder. (Indeed, we can see in the second letter that he appeals instead to marriage as the grounds for identification.)

A look at Nellie's five letters shows us some of the context that surrounded the women's dissident jokes. Living alone with an elderly and ill mother, Nellie was often stressed and ill herself, eventually leaving welding because of it. Nellie was remembered by Agnes, Emily and Ethel as a rather shy, solitary woman. Valentine's characteristically more insinuating description is that she

> was older and more sombre [than the other girls]. She probably enjoyed being with lively young people. She was tall, about forty years old, but it was hard to tell her age because she looked the same for a long time. She dressed soberly, always in blue or black. She was rather staid . . . I think the girls brought her out a lot. They were talking dirty all the time . . . Nellie tried to tag along.[56]

In this light, Nellie's parodies of the disapproval she expects for any 'bad behaviour' seem less flippant. The correspondence seems to provide a space, albeit brief, where she can explore being the 'bad daughter':

> We have had a glorious weekend together, and would not leave me till Sunday Morning. I mean under the circumstances we could not leave Mother, (but we knew where she was) (bad girl Nellie) (Letter 46)

The restricting reality of her mother's demands and conventions that define those 'circumstances' becomes clear in the next letter, in which Nellie abandons her playful style:

> Oh Miss Pearson, am worried to death, what with my work, and then had another row with Mother, that has put me back, its over Sid again, (But if you feel like writing dear, dont mention the row with Ma, she reads all my letters) His People came and brought me eggs, Strawberries, and butter, and then Ma said I made more of them than her I wish I was dead out of the way she said . . .
>
> Mother is complaining now of a pain catching her in her back, thats where I feel it being the only one, the Unemployment Place, ought never to have sent for me, leaving a woman 72, they

are never two days alike the Dr says its worry thats brought me down like this, and then the other affair.

However I must not bore you with my troubles, how is your Dad and Mother, kindly remember me to them, I only wish I had my Father, things would have been different. (Letter 49)

Here, the writing and the experiencing selves grow increasingly close and the letter seems to hover between diary and address. After a polite opening – 'Received your nice welcome letter . . .' – she descends into a monologue of worry that leads into a synchronic inscription of its cause: 'Mother is complaining now of a pain catching her in her back, that's where I feel it . . .' But paradoxically, as the letter becomes the forum for self-confession, her failure to mark any distinction between others' speech and her own seems to reflect her lack of autonomous identity. The doctor's diagnosis of 'worry', like her mother's back pain, melds into her own. Her attempt to check this in the final paragraph is unsuccessful: 'However I must not bore you with my troubles . . .' The return to the polite epistolary enquiry after Val's parents almost immediately breaks down into its association with her own lack of father, and the conditions of her present misery.

In her next and last letter, Nellie returns to her satirical drama of sexual virtue and vice, but we can now better appreciate its serious edge. The account is textured with 'spicy' dialogue and a use of the punctual present to create running commentary on the self-importance of Hopkinsons' incompetent managers:

Went to Hops last Monday and am on a Bogey-Machine, and its like your Dad says, they dont know what the devil they are doing, this machine Im on smooths off, now we have at times smoothed too much next gets tested, they all talk again, makes it too little, then, decide to send a man down to London, really I dont think they know what to do, same with drilling holes in the plates they were too small, I like it its interesting, you have plenty of Knobs to turn and push in, and I keep saying 'Harry it is stiff can you help me', he replies 'what is' then we laugh. (dirty mind you have Nellie). How are you Dear and Boy Friend, any more 'Dirty Stop Outs' (cheeky) aren't I . . . (Letter 50)

While this is interesting as a snapshot of the continuing frustrations – and pleasure – of work, what is perhaps more significant is the suggestion of the way that letter writing allows for an inner as well as outer dialogue. Her comic asides on her own narrative – 'they don't know what the devil they are doing'; 'dirty mind you have Nellie' – are the signs of experimentation with a different role, one that is 'cheeky' not only with the men at work, but with her colleagues and with Valentine too.

In a letter written around that time, Amy comments that 'Nellie is turning into a dirty girl she brought a dirty paper to us today I will copy it from her when I can find time'(Letter 32). Being a 'dirty girl' seems here to have less to do with relationships with men, than with a sense of a more independent self, in the only terms available at the time. But, as Nellie writes that self, it is just as much a literary play as a psychological one. This combination of friendship, writing and self-experiment around what we could summarise as a discourse of heterosexuality, is most developed in the correspondences of Agnes and Amy. In the following section I focus specifically on each of their correspondences in turn, before drawing some general conclusions about the kind of writing that the letters represent as a whole.

The pleasures of writing: letters from Agnes and Amy

It seems no coincidence that Agnes and Amy wrote not only the most, but the most creatively and personally. Their more complex interchange between experience, writing and corresponding is signalled by the way that they work the sexualised culture to include the letter writing itself, even more than Nellie does in her asides, making it both flirtatious and a forum for shared secrets.

Agnes Helme was the most conventionally literary of the writers, in part because she had gleaned some education beyond the age of 14, not only from her relatively educated mother and musical father but from her work as a nanny in London. On her return to Huddersfield when war broke out she took evening classes in business skills, where as well as elocution she learned 'the art of letter-writing and expression'.[57] She was also the only one of the Huddersfield group who was married at that time, and in her letters to Valentine, she is more overt about her sexual experiences. The ordinary, even painful circumstances of the day to day, welding, being married to an absent serviceman and her extremely fragile health, are employed in episodes of an ongoing shared romantic comedy – at times, bedroom farce:

My Dear Instigator of Laughs,
    I laughed untill I cried when I read your last description of the
latest adventure, of the hero, and heroine [Gottfried and Valentine]
of our most important love story. I wonder what the next
breathtaking incident will be in the next installment. (Letter 13)

Note again the parody of wartime officialese, in her revised version
of her earlier motif of the 'Laughing Motorbyke'.
    Agnes's first letter to Valentine begins with the overt proposition
of a tale. She is on a journey to Scotland to visit her husband Jack,
who was posted there, before she returns to start work at Hopkinsons.
Due to travel problems, she ends up staying in a hotel on the way,
and 'what looked like a catastrophe . . . really materialized into a
beautiful adventure'. In her exhaustion, she falls asleep on the hotel
settee, and is awoken 'with a very soft deep voice saying "Blondie
– Blondie" '. 'I sat up quickly and found myself looking rather
puzzled at the handsomest face, and the bluest eyes, I have ever seen'
(Letter 9).
    The prince-like apparition turns out to be a Canadian soldier, who
invites her to make up a party of four with him and another couple
for the evening. She accepts, and it is during the evening that she
writes the letter to Valentine. It is perhaps significant that she decides
to write at this point, as if to create her 'adventure' by invoking and
writing to her projected conspirator. As she records that the Canadian,
Eddie, admires how she scribbles away at her letter, the writing itself
becomes part of the scenario she is describing. We can imagine the
soldier watching her writing as she describes him doing so, so that
she flirts by writing as well as writing about flirting, in a classic
epistolary synchronicity of narrative and event. This draws Valentine
too into the sexual tease, as the projected other. It is underlined by
Agnes telling Valentine that she tells the GI that she is writing to
'*some* person':

Eddie has just come downstairs and pulled a wry face when he
saw me still writing, he said, 'Golly, it sure must be some letter,
and some person to whom you are writing,' I said, 'How right
you are – to both of them.' . . . if you could only hear the cracks
he is making at this letter . . . he just said if my pen was a horse
he would back it, he has never seen a pen fly like mine does.
(Letter 9)

Here she displays the hallmarks of 'epistolarity', exaggerating the letter's mediating and confidential qualities, playing off virtual relationships, of both paper and flesh, against each other. These qualities engage with the invocation of the letters as 'episodes' in an ongoing story, to gesture towards a structure of shared 'plots', pushing the letters towards narrative across the disparate moments and subjects of address.

Another running plot is that of Agnes's health. She jokes about what were evidently painful experiences, for example, the removal of her 'fangs', in a series of awful visits to the dentist. As we have seen, evidence of health problems runs throughout all the writers' letters. But Agnes's fangs seem to have a symbolic significance. Not only are they a trademark of her appearance with the other woman, but in the letters become a comic defence against sexual encounters with men:

> Speaking of your undesirable companion, I once suffered much the same sort of experience coming from Manchester to Penistone. He actually did pounce – in Woodhead tunnel, but my teeth served me well again. Jack [her husband] will be crowing when my fang does the dissapearing trick. (Letter 13)

And again:

> I'm still losing weight. I weigh 6 stone 5$\frac{1}{2}$ lbs, now. Last night I joined the paratroops, the wind lifted me completely up, and had it not been for a soldier who very obligingly was in the way of my so called flight, I might have landed in Coleridge Rd . . . He insisted he saw me home, to keep my feet on the ground. Outside our door he kissed me, and etc, but I wasn't having any. He kept murmering 'Gorgeous', in my ear, and I thought, 'Its a damn good job its blackout, if he only saw my fangs.' Anyhow I managed to get away saying I had my husband's and my chips, and they were going cold. (Letter 15)

Underlying the traumas at the dentist, and the sexual overtones of her 'fangs', Agnes's bigger worry is that she is pregnant. She makes it quite clear that she hopes that she isn't, dosing herself with gin and 'little black pills'. She describes going to Doctor Smythe:

> Jack is begging of me every letter to go to Scotland to recuperate, and I told the doctor tonight, he said 'by all means the change of

air would work wonders. My God what with a sore head, lumps,
teeth out, anticipated journeys, and er, and little bits o' things,
you really are in a way.' I blushed and answered, 'Yes! but of all
the complaints you have mentioned, the "little bits o' things" I
don't want that to go any further.' He laughed and put his arm
around my shoulders and told me I mustn't worry, all that happens
is an act of God. Thats twice he has told me that. I suppose, and
rightly so, you will be tired of hearing my complaints. (Letter 13)

As 'little bits o' things', Agnes's pregnancy is never directly mentioned
but recurs in veiled terms elsewhere in the correspondences as well
as her own. Again, such coded gossip about sexual realities – both
pleasurable and painful – produces metaphor and suspense. Amy,
for example, refers to some metonymic 'Nappies': 'Good old Aggie
getting her hand in, but it is as well she is learning how to wash
things for a start, because she might be busy washing Nappies if things
don't turn out for the better' (Letter 22). And later:

> I am going to meet Chick tonight lovely, I have not seen him all
> week but I got a letter from him yesterday, an hour from now +
> I shall be (having it) (a cuddley Woodley) Ah ah you thought I
> meant a bit of Agnes's stuff didn't you. No I could not do to be
> like her or else there would be trouble at this establishment.
> (Letter 27)

Amy's parodic reference to 'this establishment' also gives us some
idea of the benign character of the 'gossip'. As in most of them, here
Amy does not judge Agnes bad herself, but alludes to others'
judgements, most likely parents', that force circumspection and
caution. Agnes herself seems unclear as to whether it is Doctor Smythe
who is tired of hearing her complaints, or Valentine, or really, that
she herself is tired of Doctor Smythe: 'He laughed and put his arm
around my shoulders and told me I mustn't worry, all that happens
is an act of God. Thats twice he has told me that . . . '

Like Agnes, Amy Brooke found a congenial space in the
correspondence for self-creation. In fact, perhaps that space was more
unique for her than it was even for Agnes. This was not only
because Agnes had a well-to-do friend and correspondent in a
previous employer as well as Valentine, but because subsequent
interviewing has revealed a significant gap between the way that Amy
represented herself in the letters and the way that she was perceived
and is now remembered by the other welders, a point to which I

shall return in the Epilogue. Amy was less educated than Agnes, and her style is less literary. But here too, letter writing involves a kind of flirtation. Despite, or perhaps because of, the more literal conception of writing, Amy is attuned to the dimension of the letter as object as well as text, potential fetish as well as communication. She says that Nellie, who we may remember is sick in bed, wants her to 'lay on the bed beside her, but I have refused, but tomorrow I will get in, and press your note into her bosom'. On another occasion, she also invokes the physical participation of the letter in their fantasies:

> My dear Vagrant,
> Hello you dirty stay-out all night, under Hedgebottoms, in tents, and now in Lavatories where will it be next? jail I should imagine. Ha Ha to think I was under the impression you was spending a week away again, when I did not hear from you all last week, anyway my letter spent a dirty night out instead of coming to Sheepridge [where Amy lived]. (Letter 32)

Lack of punctuation does not prevent the inscription of revealing thought processes through shifts in imagery and register. In the following monologic flow, such shifts are weighted with more serious dilemmas:

> We have spent a marvellous evening together last Friday honestly speaking lots of love was not in the running he was lovely I bet he will be mad when he gets my letter putting him off tomorrow. He is still very much in love, it is his Birthday a week on Wednesday but I don't know what he wants there is one thing he does want more than anything (real love) ha ha I am going to give in though before long if things don't alter at Hopkinsons I am just in the mood maybe it is as well I am not seeing him tomorrow because I should not hesitate to let him (have it) I dont give a bugar what happens nowadays I absolutely loath Hopkinsons anyway as far as gas cutting is concerned I am definately not stopping on that machine I AM GOING WELDING they have upset the applecart this week. (Letter 29)

The transformation of being 'in the mood' to loathing Hopkinsons here underlines the sexual restrictions a woman faced, then, where the price of 'real love' was jeopardising your job through risk of pregnancy. 'I AM GOING WELDING' contradicts 'I dont give a bugar what happens nowadays', a contradiction that makes it plain how little she enjoys that restriction.

More often though, the effect of Amy's associative style is of pleasure and intimacy, overflowing boundaries:

> I hope [Agnes's] Sweetheart gets some digs for her, and then maybe her will be able to finish the job off right, and bring forth fruits.
>
> Talking about fruit, I have just had some prunes for my sweet tonight and I was reading your letter at the same time, and did I laugh. I think mine would be much sweeter than yours, because the day I wet myself, with laughing, I had some Prunes up my knickers slop, and I threw them under the saw somewhere, but I am in good condition so you will not be poisoned. (Letter 22)

Her dry-humoured changes of register from the everyday 'job' of having a baby to the quasi-biblical 'bringing forth fruits' and then to the prunes she had for her sweet, express the same casual critique of the powers that make babies, struggle and hard work, working women's lot that we have seen throughout the letters. But these sweets, laughter, fruit, wetting, are also bacchanalian games. Amy seems to make a motif of fruit the way Agnes does of her teeth: 'I have lost a lot of weight lately and yesterday I had my ulcer pains again was it the plums or the pears or was it love? what do you think (ha ha)' (Letter 29). The range between romance and realism, sometimes comically immediate, show the letters as a space for 'Aimeee' both to write herself into Hollywood, 'making violent love in the shop doorway next to the Picturedrome' (Letter 32), as well as to moan prosaically that 'as for Amy well I have some liver to cook for supper . . . and I am to wash yet believe me I am bugared' (Letter 34).

These letters from Agnes and Amy were the first of what turned out to be life-long correspondences with Valentine. For them, writing was clearly a pleasure in itself.[58] Consider the following quotation from Agnes:

> I feel I could sit and write and write and better write, just as I loved to stand and talk to you, but although I have not told you all I should have liked, I really must make my Allenbury's Food, (builds bonny babies) and go to bed it is very very late. (Letter 13)

It is notable that writing is like 'standing and talking', suggesting that for her, letters are like conversation. But it is crucial that we do not simply read the letters as transcriptions or extensions of speech. Agnes is also exploring the distinctive pleasure of writing, which is generated as much by internal momentum ('write and write and better write'), as by the wish to 'tell all'. This momentum characterises all of her letters, most obviously in her inability to sign off without numerous farewell wishes, jokes, afterthoughts and postscripts. Amy too testifies to the dynamic, in a second postscript:

> Note paper seems to be going with a swing hear tonight I had no idea I had written you so much but maybe you will write a bit more next time. I hope so because I soon read through tonights. My mother wants to know if I am hear for the night. I guess I could go on all night if I told you all that went off at work anyway I dont like to bore you so I will ring off. Harold has gone to Ilkley until Sunday so I will give him your love when he comes home. He seems to be like me looking for letters from you he was asking me why you had not written on Tuesday he said had you crossed me off I told him he knew as much about you as I did. Cheerio Love. Excuse Pencil in a hurry. (Letter 29)

This double, and contradictory, aesthetic is a classic paradox of the epistolary genre. Critic Louise Horowitz notes that 'the ideal vehicle for communication of the passions allowing for the greatest *vraisemblance* (with "I" and "you" linked directly), the letter, like the journal, is also the intense consciousness of writing' (6). As Horowitz suggests, we must not read the letters' 'communication of the passions' or 'vraisemblance', too literally.

The content and the style of the correspondence cannot easily be separated. It is difficult, for example, to say whether Agnes wrote with such style in part because she was relieved to find a confidante for taboo subjects, or whether she was interested in confiding because she enjoyed writing so much. But maybe this is a false opposition. Rather, it would seem that the particular relationship that she struck with Valentine, one in which she wished to impress or entertain, produced a particular version of self. That self teeters between bravado and braveness, but is essentially comic and powerful. This is most strikingly highlighted if we look at the letters she wrote around this time, to her husband, who was posted in Scotland.[59] Here not only does she represent herself as dependent and depressed, but she shows none of the inventiveness of style. In the following letter, she tells him her fear that she is pregnant:

I am sitting in front of a lovely fire in our room, writing this, I hope you are just as comfortable. There is only two things worrying me. One is, I have toothache again, will I be damed glad, when I have them out, and secondly, for two days, I have had a stiff neck, and earache, and tonight, whilst washing my neck I found a hard lump just behind my ear in my hair. It is very sore, and I don't know what it is. I shall go to the nurse tomorrow if it is no better. Another thing – I havn't got Granny yet, and I have been very billious twice, I don't know what to think. Anyhow, I shall give myself another two days, and if not then, I shall do something. Mother is locking up, so I must only write a few more minutes. Thanks for your letters darling mine. They really do me good, when I come home tired at nights to find a letter. There is part of the letter I received today, I can't read at all. I do wish you would take a little more time with your writing, then you wouldn't scribble so much. Dearest, all I want to write to you is, I love you, love you, love you, love you, and come home, come home come home, come home, like broken records over and over again, but it sounds so silly when you actually put it down, and so I find myself writing anything but what my heart wants me to write, and only the things my head says.

I have some bad news. Our Tom sails for the East in a day or two, I was very upset when I read his letter. Oh this cruel cruel war, breaking up that happy family circle, of theirs, and smashing all to Hell, the brilliant future he had before him, but if I know our Tom, he will come through alright, he's the type. God speed him to safety. Darling I hope you never leave me – never, especially if its true I'm pregnant.

. . . You ask about my work no, I still am not welding, we are doing anything to pass time on. Well my darling I will say Goodnight my love till tomorrow. I won't close this letter as I will write some more at work tomorrow, so Goodnight and God bless love That is what you always say, but only once did you follow it with, 'I love you darling.' do you remember? I do . . . Goodnight sweetheart may God go with you. xxxxxx

. . . I hope I shall shortly be coming up again, and I shall be very happy just to be with you my sweet. My life is my love for you, and knowing that whatever happens, at least I can be sure of one who will stand by me. Darling I really think there is a little life of yours springing into being.

I am going to the doctors in the morning, I am missing my work. I am longing for you more than ever now, God! how I long to feel safe in your arms again. I love to have your arms around me darling, I then forget everything but just we two. Hurry home, darling home to me. Happy the day when you come home never to return. Goodbye by sweet husband all my love to you, and God be with you. Cheerio my love. Darling I am crying, I do wish you were here I miss you so. Agnes.

ps. The money is for the shirts. Please let me know immediately you receive it.[60]

As in her letters to Valentine, she wraps her most important health worry, her possible pregnancy, in her other health problems, here almost as an afterthought to the only 'two things that are worrying her'. The meaning of the local phrase 'I havn't got Granny yet' becomes more obvious later in the letter, but the moment at which it returns is significant. In both cases, it follows elevated statements about separation, the war, and her love for him, in a sudden drop in style from self-consciously rhetorical to emotional. Particularly striking is the contrast between her confident statement that her brother will 'come through' the war, and her following fearful hope that Jack will not leave her. But although she clearly wants him to stand by her, she does not ask his advice, saying only obliquely that she will 'do something', if it is true she is pregnant.

The style of the letter is more 'diaristic' than in the letters to Valentine. But it appears to struggle with the grandiose discourse of 'keeping up the morale' that women were expected to write in their letters to 'our boys'. Women writing to men in the services typically faced a double bind of representing themselves as both newly self-sufficient and still ultimately dependent on their absent man, clearly, an awkward and ironic position. This was in part the natural result of wanting to protect the other from worry, but it also reflected the ideology that, we have seen, demanded women be independent only 'for the duration'.[61] Agnes struggles with this here, at the expense of representing her own most pressing communication.[62] The pleasures of letter writing are far more elusive.

Writing and friendship

If we compare the correspondence in this book to the letters that women wrote to absent men, or to their mothers, which were the kinds of letters published during the war, they are strikingly original. Nevertheless, we must not exaggerate the radical edge to the correspondence. Neither Valentine nor her trainees saw the relationship as an equal one. Furthermore, that the welders articulate self-making as primarily sexual suggests how limited these terms of self-representation remained. The very fact that most of the writers chose not to continue writing may be related to discomfort with these terms. The limitations of a common language of heterosexuality are shown most clearly by the hypothetical silence of any lesbian confidences. This is not entirely an anachronistic question, since Valentine herself declares that one of the group was excluded by the others because they felt she had lesbian tendencies. Perhaps more representative is Emily's decision to stop at one 'thank you' letter. Although Emily lets 'Miss Pearson' in on the gossip, she is not sure whether to construct herself as one of Valentine's 'bad girls' or not:

> [Nellie's mother] thinks Amy and I are two grand girls, you had better put her wise, and another thing I should just like to know why I need watching, I can assure you I have not commited any dark and deadly deeds nor slept underneath hedges, nor any that is wrong. (Letter 40)

Notice how her about-face 'assurance' of her virtue produces a shift in vocabulary, ending in the more formal register of 'nor any that is wrong'. This language of a gentlewoman wrongly accused faintly evokes the ironic reversal that here the genteel woman is less virtuous than the working one, suggesting an even more satirical ambiguity in the term 'good girl'.

In sum, Valentine encouraged sexual independence within the conventional expectations of heterosexuality, femininity and eventual marriage. The most that could be said of this as resistance was solidarity within an acceptance of an age-old 'sex war', which was not reconceived in any new way. This isn't so very different from women's peacetime allegiances. Studies of adolescent girls today show that they use heterosexual intrigue to make friends with each other, and any look at women's magazines shows that the interest in 'getting', 'keeping' or 'pleasing' a man paradoxically forms the basis for the biggest 'women's club' in the world. War affects this only in that it exaggerates the same structures of sexual difference, creating a society obsessed with sexual segregation and reunion.[63] In my interview with Valentine, she described feminism as 'pretty silly, for the most part':

MJ: So you don't think [the war] was a time of – it didn't turn you into a feminist, or anyone else?

VP: No, it was just a fact of survival. And really there was a few times during the war when it could easily have gone the other way.

MJ: How do you mean?

VP: We'd have lost. And then, England would have been taken over and then we'd have been in a much worse situation. People would really have been told what to do. I mean there would have been no choice.

In this way, the letters' dramatisation of a solidarity and pleasure between women remains very much within the terms of the period. Despite their differences, the women shared with Valentine a destiny in which they were all expected to support their 'heroes', obey their fathers, to marry, to bear children. Yet, the unfinished, momentary character of the letter leaves the public reader with a sense of the individual interpretations of those expectations. More striking still, it foregrounds the creative possibilities of relationship between women, both in life and in writing.

III   People in the Letters

Penistone

Helena Marsh (later Varley) – welder at David Brown
Dorothy Roebuck (later Adams) – welder at David Brown
Joan Baines (née Thorpe) – welder at David Brown
Violet Champion (later Jessop) – welder at David Brown

Huddersfield

Leonora Agnes Helme (née Green) nicknamed Fanny Four Rod –
    welder at Hopkinsons
Jack Helme – Agnes's husband
Frank (Daddy) Helme – her father-in-law
Ma Helme – mother-in-law
Pat Green – sister
Tom Green – brother
Edna Green – sister
Fan – relative of Agnes, married to Kathleen

Ron (Gordon) – Agnes's singing partner

Amy Brooke (later Hargate) nicknamed the Mighty Atom – welder
    at Hopkinsons
Harold Brooke – brother
Frank Brooke – brother
Evelyn Brooke – elder sister
Hilda Brooke – elder sister
Chick – boyfriend
Frank – boyfriend
Harry – boyfriend
Alec – Evelyn's husband

Ethel (later Kergon) – welder at Hopkinsons
John Kergon – fiancé, later husband

Jenny (last name not known) – welder at Hopkinsons

Eleanor Hardcastle (Nellie) – welder at Hopkinsons
Sidney – Nellie's boyfriend

Alice Burden – welder at Hopkinsons

Emily Castle (née Jones) – welder at Hopkinsons
Norman Castle – Emily's fiancé, later husband

Enid Hiley (maiden name not known) – welder at Hopkinsons
Cyril Hiley – Enid's boyfriend, later husband

Mrs Marflit – supervisor
Willie Brooks – disliked foreman
Sydney Wright – works manager
Arthur – foreman
Stanley Robinson – well-liked foreman
Eddie – a co-worker
Chris – a co-worker

Sheffield

Valentine Pearson (later Morche) – welding trainer at Welding
    Rods Ltd
Gottfried Morche – Valentine's boyfriend, later husband

Mr Pearson – Valentine's father and Managing Director of Welding
  Rods

Dorothy – secretary at Welding Rods

Margaret – Welding Rods employee

Walter – Welding Rods employee

Audrey – probably payroll

John Bull – foreman (much nicknamed)

Mr and Mrs Holmes – policeman and his wife with whom most
  Huddersfield women were billeted

Mrs Feather – nickname for the owner of the sweet shop the women
  went to

The Letters

I Enjoying the War: Letters from Helena Marsh, Dorothy Roebuck, Joan Baines and Violet Champion

Helena Marsh (later Varley) was born on 23 December 1919. She left school at 14, working in a rug mill and then a bakery, until she joined David Brown in 1939 when she was 20. She was the third of six children. Her father worked in the gas works, was briefly unemployed, and then worked for the local council. Her mother worked in service in hotels until she was married.

1 Fully skilled and willing working welders

52 Park Avenue,
Penistone,
N Sheffield,
Yorks

March 1942

Dear Miss Pearson,

I hope you'll forgive me for not writing before now, but here I am at last, trying to put a few lines together. Dorothy received your letter this morning. She came into work for 2.00 p.m. this afternoon and let Violet and I read it. I didn't know you had some girls from Huddersfield learning welding. It's to be hoped they behave better than we did, but by all accounts they're just as bad.

I suppose you'll have heard about the lovely big wages we're getting now. The times we've been in the offices since Christmas I wouldn't care to count, and after all our efforts, we get a 5/- rise. I wish they would rise me out of the firm for good. I drew for a week's wage £1-16-0 last week of course stoppages off, but how do they expect a girl to live on that a week? After my board is paid I've hardly enough to keep me in cigs. I wish we could get a job in Sheffield, welding of course, where there would be more money and more work, as we have hardly anything to do. Last week [Violet] and I were working the 2–10 shift and after 5 O'clock we had to do core-making, so you can tell how busy we are welding. If you could tell us, Miss Pearson, of any firms in Sheffield wanting girl welders we would see what could be done about us being released from this dump of David Brown's. We are all fond of our job of welding, and I, for one wouldn't like to give it up.

I hope you don't think I'm mad about work, but I'm telling you just plain facts, and hope my letter won't bore you.

Violet and I are having a good time just now. We have gone about together since we were at Sheffield. We've gone to all dances and the places where one always gets merry, and have we been merry? I'll say we have. By the way Violet wants remembering to you, and wants you to have a pint for us in the old 'Salutation Inn'.

I suppose you'll have heard about me at Joan's wedding. Well I was drinking neat rum and was flat out for above 2 hours and was I feeling bad the next day.

Well, Miss Pearson, I haven't given you much gushing news, but that's all I can think of just now. Please remember me to Dorothy and the nice young blonde in the office, I think Margaret is her name, but I'm not sure. So I'll sign off now hoping to hear from you soon.

Cheerio for now,
Yours sincerely,
Helena

P.S. Please, don't forget to let us know if there are any firms in Sheffield wanting <u>fully skilled</u> and <u>willing working</u> welders. I Thank You.

Dorothy Roebuck (later Adams) was born 14 March 1923. One of eight children, she left school at 14 to work as a day girl doing housework. In 1941, aged 18, she went to work at David Brown as a core-maker, and in 1942 worked as a welder after training in Sheffield. Her father was the first insurance agent in Penistone for the travel company, Thomas Cook, after having worked as a train driver.

2 'I bet you painted Sheffield red'

135 Green Road,
Penistone,
Yorks

27 February 1942

Dear Miss Pearson,

Just a line to let you know I am still living and have not forgotten how good you were to us when we were at Welding Rods Lmt. Joan lets me read her letters from you.

I am going to her wedding tomorrow. I bet she'll make a lovely bride, don't you? She had been worried as to whether Ernest would be able to get [here] or not, but she got a telegram to say that he had got a 48 hrs pass. You should of seen her face.

As I suppose you'll know that Helena and Vi are on the opposite shift to us, so we don't see much of them.

I hope you had a nice time when your boy came home on leave. I bet you painted Sheffield red. I would like to take this opportunity of thanking you for the nice Xmas cards you sent me.

If ever I am in Sheffield and have a bit of time to spare I'll call in and see you. I did not hear anything about that spot of bother so don't be worried about it.

Love to all at W.R.S.[1]
Dot

---

[1] Welding Rods, Sheffield.

3   *The burns aren't fatal*

135 Green Road,
Penistone

16 March 1942

Dear Val,

Thanks for your letter of the ninth, it was nice hearing from you after not seeing you for so long.

We seem to be getting along alright without fatal burns but get a few round our eyes. Joan and I are on 6–2 this week but are changing a shift for Vi and Helena tomorrow so that they can go to a dance. I am going to one on Friday and have got a nice new dress for the occasion. My Mother bought it me for my birthday.

By the way we don't get any overtime in. We work five shifts one week and six another. When Joan got married, two of us went upstairs and made a lovely apple pie bed, you know, one of those you can't get into. Anyway, they must have been ticked off about it and remade it. Someone else sewed their pyjamas up and they were ages unpicking them. If I'd been in Joan's place I don't think I'd have bothered, would you?

My sister has got a post in a Royal Ordnance Factory at Thorp Arch near Leeds. She likes that kind of nursing better than the other. She works three eight hour shifts whereas we only work two. She's courting a metallurgist from Brown's, a nice lad too although he's far from being as good looking as Frank Beamer. From all accounts, he's not much cop.

Vi and Helena think I've reformed because I haven't been to many dances lately and don't go out with them on pub crawls. Well for one thing I am not of age. For another, Penistone is a small place and one can easily get one's name up.

The weather is not too bad here. The snow has practically gone now, thank goodness!

Joan and I are going to the pictures tonight, so give my love to all at WR.

Love,

Dot x

P.S. Don't think I'm scrounging for the C.I.S. It's one of Dad's envelopes.

P.P.S. It's a crack back at you for the bill you sent.[2]

---

[2] Valentine had used an old tax office envelope for her last letter, so Dot used a Crown Information Service one back.

4   *Chocolate and cigarettes from an airman*

135 Green Road,
Penistone,
Yorks

29 April 1942

Dear Val,

Thanks for your letter that I received the other day, it's nice to hear from you occasionally. Yes I do know Aggie Green, but don't call her Aggie to her face for God's sake, or she'll have a fit. She only used to live about thirty yards from us. She used to sing in local concerts when she was a kid, you know the type – 'Ours is a nice house ours is' and 'I like apples and plums'. I can picture her now. Legs like a canary and prominent teeth.

I wouldn't like to be in your place now Val, trying to teach six people to weld in that welding place, especially if they are half so noisy and talkative as we were. If we want to talk to anybody now it's got to be ourselves.[3]

Joan and I are going to the pictures tonight. My <u>air force boyfriend</u> is on duty tonight. I know what you will be thinking – 'Fancy Dot going off the straight and narrow and going out with strange boys', I'm still thinking it. It's very convenient for me because he brings me cigarettes and chocolate every time I go out with him. He can't be married because he has pots of dough.

By the way Val, how is your fiancé getting on and are you being true to him? I don't think you would be if you came to Penistone just now, lots of soldiers and airmen, not forgetting the local talent.

I bet you didn't have your gas mask ready the other day when the curtain was on fire, or you would have dashed in with that on.[4] And Walter, my heart-throb, ha ha! with his centre parting, dashing to the rescue.[5] Isn't Joan's husband a grand lad? I've told her I could fall for him in a big way myself.

---

[3] At first there were only six women from Hopkinsons, since Nellie and Agnes came later.

[4] Valentine must have described the incident when the curtain caught fire during the Huddersfield women's training. The incident was remembered as a good story because Alice had tried to put out the fire with a bucket of oil (thinking it was water), described in Agnes's poem 'The Sparks'. (See Preface.)

[5] Walter, an employee at Welding Rods, was clearly the butt of some jokes, although not disliked as John Bull was.

Cilla still likes her job but, alas, I think the love bug has bitten her. 'Ain't it sickening this ere love business.' I don't know if I told you or not, but our Henry is a daddy again. You can't keep a good man down, can you. The baby's name is Susan. She's eight weeks old and she's a little picture.

Well Val, that's all my news for the present so will close, Oh! the others send their love and remember me to Dorothy.[6]

Lots of love,

Dorothy

---

[6] Dorothy was an employee at Welding Rods.

5 *The girls from Hopkinsons are lucky blighters*

135 Green Road,
Penistone,
Yorks

13 July 1942

Dear Val,

Thanks for your letter, which I have been so long in answering. Glad to hear that the girls from Hopkinsons are behaving themselves, but aren't they staying a long time? Lucky blighters.

Joan's husband has gone to Northern Ireland and Joan and I are having a good time. I can't believe that she's married yet. We went to a dance last night. Helena seemed to be doing alright with the army.

We are still not working overtime. We have only worked two Sundays since we went on the job. At present we haven't enough work to keep us going. It's our holidays the week after next, so don't be surprised if I walk in to see you. Vi is going to Blackpool, and Joan is going to stay with her Auntie for the week, I am going to Warrington for a day or two and then going to different places on the days I have left.

Joan and I gave a pint of blood last Monday, to be sent to the Navy. The sailor that gets my blood will be a lad if he isn't already.

Dad was 65 yesterday, but he is keeping on working, and will also get his pension. By the way we had some men from Hopkinsons at Brown's last week. Give my love to Dorothy and Margaret.

How's your fiancé getting on, is he still in England? Well Val, I think that this is all the news for the present so will close now.

Lots of love,
Dorothy

Joan Baines (née Thorpe) was born in 1922. She was one of two children, with a half-sister from her father's later marriage. She left school at 14 to work in a laundry. Her father and brother worked at David Brown which she joined in the early years of the war as a core-maker. She began welding in 1942, the year that she married Ernest Baines.

6 Demanding better pay

41, Church Hill,
Penistone

. Thursday [February 1942]

Dear Val,

Thanks for your letter which I received last Wednesday. I'm sorry I haven't written to you earlier but time has been very scarce this last week or two.

Ernest has just been over to tell me he is going to Scotland on his Air Gunners course on Saturday. So I shall not see him so often as I have been doing lately. To make things worse we were getting married at the end of the month and now we don't know how he'll get over. Everything is arranged for the wedding, I've got my clothes, which of course are white and the bridesmaids have theirs. Also the first calling of the banns have been read. Furthermore quite a few out of the forces are coming and have managed to change their leaves over so they can get [here]. Really this is a rotten mess to be in, so we are hoping he can get home.

Now for work. Violet is off work and under the doctor too. She was doing some burning out[7] and it seems she nearly burnt her foot out instead of the casting.

Dot last night, while coming home from the flicks, went head-first into a snow drift and ended up with cauliflower ear, so she's off work until Monday also. She's going to the doctor's as well. Seems this doctor will be doing a roaring trade. Helena is OK, and so am I, but I don't know how long. I hope you're doing alright.

Oh by the way, have you got your book back which you lent Jack A?[8] You know he's left our place about 3 weeks ago and I kept reminding him. He managed to get his release papers through

---

[7] The women at Brown's were largely employed on repair work of imperfect castings.

[8] This may have been a pass-book, which Valentine used to travel with.

alright. Now he's somewhere round Pontefract, welding gasometers or something.

We got our rate of pay altered, for we kept at them until they saw to the matter.[9]

Are you going alright with the girls from Huddersfield? It will be rather a tight squeeze getting six of them onto two welding sets.

I've had my neck burnt and side of my face since I came back. There is still the trade mark on my neck though.

Thanks a lot for the invitation of letting me come any time I want to see you. I will come when I'm in Sheffield but I couldn't say when that will be.

Anyhow I'll let you know how things turn out for my future.

Hoping for the best, I remain,

Yours,

Joan

P.S. Have any of the others wrote yet, they said they were going to.

[9] See p. 20 for a discussion of their struggle for equal pay.

7   *A wartime wedding*

41 Church Hill,
Penistone

5 March 1942

Dear Val,

Thanks for the letter, but forgive me for not answering sooner. Well I got married last Saturday the 28th Feb., so now I've gone and spoilt my manners. He managed to get a 48 hr pass from Walney Island. That's off Barrow in Furness where he is now stationed. So we only had one night together, for he had to go back the next day.

I think everyone who came enjoyed themselves, for they'd plenty to eat and drink. I would have liked you to have come but I couldn't let you know in time. You see I didn't get to know properly until Friday dinnertime, so what could I have done? Never mind, I'm sending a small piece of wedding cake. We couldn't get any almonds, so we had just to make do with icing sugar.[10] The service was quite nice. As I came in the organist played 'Here comes the bride'; then before we started with the marriage service we had the hymn sung 'The voice that breathed o'er Eden'. As we were walking up to the altar the organ played 'Handel's Largo', then coming out of the church the other wedding march was played. Of course we had our photographs taken and I got the proofs today so maybe when I get the proper photos I'll send one along of Ernest and myself.

Work isn't going down too bad, and good to say I never get bored with welding. We haven't had much to do this week so I've been doing rather a lot of reading. The others are OK. Violet and Helena got canned on Saturday at the wedding. Dot said she was going to write this week, so I hope she has done. Are the girls from Huddersfield still at Sheffield and how are they doing? I'm glad Jack Allen sent your book back. Tell Dot I hope she's much better and things are going fine with her. I'm glad to hear your fiancé came over, and I sincerely hope he comes often.

The weather here just now is lousy, knee deep in snow and drifts all over the place. I'll tell you I'm fed up with the sight of snow, it's coming down like anything, and I was hoping it would clear for the weekend. What hopes.

[10] 'Make do and mend'-style weddings, with dresses made of parachute silk and no marzipan for the cake, are often motifs of women's wartime memories.

Well Val, I'll have to sign off now, for I've some more letters to write tonight.

So take care of yourself and write when you have time, for I like to hear from you.

Your Friend,

Joan

P.S. My name is Mrs E. Baines and it is still the same address.

Violet Champion (later Jessop) was born in Penistone on 29 March
1920. She had one brother and sister. Her father worked on the
railways. She began work in the core-shop at Brown's in 1938 aged
18, before training as a welder.

8 *Have a good time before you get married*

41 Park Avenue,
Penistone,
Yorks

Tuesday, 10 March 1942

Dear Miss Pearson,
          I am sorry I have not wrote to you before but with being
on shifts it was too much trouble to come home and then start letter
writing.
          Well how are you getting on at Sheffield? Still OK? I just
wish you lived up here as Helena and I are having a grand time, and
we often say when we go for a drink that it would be nice if you
could be with us. Anyway, when you go out for one, just have one
for us, will you?
          We went to Joan's wedding last Saturday and she did look
nice all in white. And, oh boy, did we have some fun. Helena had
one over the eight and went flat out. It was about 11 p.m. when
she went out so we had to let her sleep it off. I waited till she came
round. It was then 2.30 a.m. Sunday morning and if you could have
seen us going up the road you would have split your side with
laughing. And the thing that she kept saying to me, it just reminded
me of that Friday when we left Sheffield.
          Dot was disgusted at us and said we let the welders down.
I don't know whether Dot has told you or not, but she has turned
teetotal. So I have been pulling her leg and I said it would be no
good her com[ing] to Sheffield with us unless she could drink.
When the weather gets nice again you bet your life that we shall
come and see you then, we can have a good night out. I have some
good tales to tell you when I do see you. Well Val, I hope you don't
mind me calling you that? but how is your boy friend getting on
with Army life? Do you know we have been looking for a letter to
say that you were getting married. But no fear, I think you are like
Helena and I, you want a good time first.

Well now I would just like to thank both you and your father for what you have done for us. I think you were very good indeed and I hope if ever there is anything that we are not sure about in welding we can come to you for advice.

Well I don't think I have any more news so keep smiling and all the best,

From your friend,
Vi

P.S. Hope to hear from you soon.

II   The Romance of Letter-writing: Letters from Agnes Green, 'Fanny Four Rod'

Leonora Agnes Green was born in 1917 in Penistone, Yorkshire. She was the next to youngest of nine children, of whom seven survived. The family were known locally for their musical and dramatic activities. Her father, 'Piccolo Tom', was a railway ganger; her mother, though not in paid work, sometimes did sewing. Agnes sang musical comedy as part of 'the Green Sisters', before she followed two of her brothers to London at the age of 15. Here she went into service as a child's nanny but she 'got so ragged for the way she spoke' (a Yorkshire accent) that she came home and took elocution and secretarial lessons. Returning to London, she worked as a nanny again for Mrs Shah, who became a life-long friend. Due to ill health, Agnes returned for a brief visit to her family, who had moved to Huddersfield. During the visit, the war broke out so she stayed, working in the family shop. She began courting Jack Helme, who was five years her junior, in 1941, and on his leave in January 1942 they were married, despite initial opposition from her mother. In February she arrived in Sheffield with Jack, to begin training as a welder for Hopkinsons. Her first letter is written *en route* for Inverary, where she was going for a holiday to see Jack and recuperate from illness.

9   A wartime journey

On the back of this letter Agnes has written:
RESERVE THIS FOR ANY CASE OF EMERGENCY.

> c/o Mrs Peel
> 4, Leckon Terrace,
> Furnes,
> Argyllshire
> Scotland
>
> [late July 1942]

My Dear Friend,
          I have put my prospective heading to my letter, but here it is Saturday night, and I am still in Glasgow. I am residing at some Hotel, I forget its name, but what looked like a catastrophe, has really materialised into a beautiful adventure. One I could well imagine you to be the participant of. Here, as near as I can tell you, are the details. I left Huddersfield at 11-15 last night, and I found Daddy

Helme[11] had put me into the wrong train. Rectifying that mistake, I eventually started my journey. Arriving in Manchester, the Glasgow Train was filled to capacity, so consequently, there were about 30 of us, stranded. We were placed in a train to Wigan, but when we arrived at Wigan, we were still unable to board the train for Scotland. We were waiting for a train to Preston, when I jumped on, and asked if I was right for Preston. The guard very brusquely said, 'Hell no, this train is non-stop to Glasgow'. Imagine my joy, when quite by accident I had boarded the correct train. The journey was long, and tedious, and it was 10.45 a.m. before we arrived at Glasgow. I parked my case, and I went in search of this elusive bus station Jack had spoken of so often. I was directed to one, I was told to go to another. I retraced my steps, and arriving at the second bus station for the bus to Furness, the inspector said 'There are only two buses, you have missed the morning bus, and the next is 4.50.' Jack had said it was 3.15, but the man said it was 4.50. I nearly bought Lewis's in the course of this day, walking in sheer exasperation to the bus station, − only to my chagrin to find my bus had gone at 3.15. Imagine what I felt like stranded in Glasgow. I let that inspector have it I can tell you, and then he said 'I told you where to catch your bus,' which he never did. I eventually dissolved into tears, and as plainly as I could, I told a policeman my story.

The policeman and the sergeant brought me to this Hotel to secure me a night's lodging. They have managed to squeeze me in. The son here is charming (just as I was writing that he came in to tell me my room was no. 18). He also said he would like to take me for a glimpse of the Clyde when he is finished his work, but I told him I was going to bed. He said I had a comfortable bed − a single one, and he would stand guard at my door all night to make sure I was safe. Anyway to continue my running commentary. After I had been signed in, I sat on a settee, and before I knew what had happened − I was asleep. I was really fatigued. I awoke with a very soft deep voice saying 'Blondie − Blondie'. I sat up quickly and found myself looking, rather puzzled, at the handsomest face, and the bluest eyes, I have ever seen. In my confusion, I thought it was the son, but as I apologised for falling asleep, he said, 'Please don't − I have only just come down from bed myself'. So I knew I had not met him before. We conversed quite naturally − and I soon learned he was a Canadian. We became quite friendly, and soon we were joined with still another Canadian. Before I knew what had happened, I was having tea with them. Their names are Eddie, and Robert, respectively. Robert was meeting a lady friend, and I am going with Eddie − (my

[11] Her father-in-law, Frank Helme.

blue-eyed boy) – to make the foursome. Am I really wicked? I can't help but keep thinking what Jack is wondering and doing right now. He will be worried about me I know. I would rather be with him than here but I might as well make the best of a bad job.

Eddie has just come downstairs and pulled a wry face when he saw me still writing. He said, 'Golly, it sure must be some letter, and some person to whom you are writing'. I said, 'How right you are – to both of them'. Anyway I will finish this later.

If I make any mistakes now blame it on the scotch and sodas I have had, and the piano player right behind me. It is 10.30, and I feel just fit for anything.

Eddie, is really something, yes here it comes, I'm fascinated to death with his eyes, and his truly cross-atlantic drawl, which seems to come right from his boots. If you could only hear the cracks he is making at this letter, he is making Pauline cry with laughing. He just said if my pen was a horse he would back it, he has never seen a pen fly like mine does. By the way he still calls me 'Blondie'.

Charlie (the son) has just been to me and sarcastically asked me if I'd enjoyed my night in bed. I said 'Certainly I had', but his anger was assumed, for he called me Flower, and chucked me under the chin. I wonder which flower I remind people of. It must be a cow slop.

I have never seen anything as fascinating as a scotchman in kilts. I was watching four this afternoon as if I had never seen a scotchman before. The swing of their kilt, their legs, and bits o' things are not to be sneezed at. (They could be if they had pepper on.) Well dear, I really must close now, and join the company. Don't forget to give my best regards to Mr Pearson, Dorothy, and Walter, not forgetting John Thomas Buffalo.[12] Please convey my thanks to Mr Pearson for the lovely day I had last Tuesday.[13] I've had a card from Ethel. Goodbye and God Bless You. I am just going onto the piano.[14]

Goodnight and best of luck.

I Remain Yours,

Agnes

Please don't forget to let me know how my tubes went on. 115 and 117. Love Leo.[15]

---

[12] The Welding Rods crowd.

[13] This may refer to a well-remembered outing in which Valentine and her father Mr Pearson took Amy and Agnes for what they thought would be a genteel meal out, but which involved a hearty traipse across the moors.

[14] Agnes was used to performing.

[15] The 'tubes' were test-pieces of welds that were sent out from Welding Rods to be tested for tensile strength. The numbers identify Agnes's pieces. 'Leo' is short for Leonora, her first name.

10   *The truth about the war effort*

9 Station Road,
Milnsbridge,
Hudds

[early August 1942]

My Dear Laughing Motorbyke.,
        I hope you are having no trouble in acquiring your petrol
ration, because should you have to garage your laugh, you would
hardly be the same person, at least to me. As you see by my letter
head, I am back home, putting my shoulder to the wheel, and what
a wheel. I sincerely, though regretfully state, it is badly in need of
oiling. I have never been so disgusted in my life at the disgraceful
way Hopkinsons Ltd is managed. We are <u>not</u> welding, we are
pushed from pillar to post, and today, after asking the foreman for
a job, he said, 'Just stand there in that corner'. That was at 7.45 at
the latest, and at 3.15 in the afternoon, I was still standing in my
corner. In desperation, I walked over to where Ethel and Jenny were
painting. I very unconcerned sat down, and started, when who should
come pompously down, but Grandmother Marflitt. 'What are you
doing there?' said she, 'who gave you permission to sit there?' I very
steadily looked at her and said, 'I gave it to myself'. I then told her
I had been standing in a corner all day, and she promised to speak
to Willie Brooks. Nevertheless, neither of them came, and I went
there too, today, and nothing was said. They are still setting girls
on, and there is insufficient work for the ones already employed.
I'm afraid [if] the truth was known about the actual facts, of the
slackness of the workers, and the incompetence of its bosses – there
would be trouble. We can smoke all day, and talk all day to our
fellow workers – even leaving our machines to do it, and nothing
is said. I feel like saying a lot, I can tell you, and had I known a week
ago what I know now, wild elephants would not have fetched me
home from Scotland, war effort, or no war effort. Why the devil I
couldn't stay at Sheffield, I don't know, and Marflitt said we should
have to come back to Sheffield for a fortnight to get in trim again.
Anyway one thing – Mrs Holmes wouldn't know me these days.[16]
7.10 Tues, 7.10 Thurs: what do you think of that? I told you I could
get up when occasion demanded. (Touch wood.)

---

[16] Agnes was billeted with Mr and Mrs Holmes in Sheffield. Clearly she was not
   keen on early rising.

9 Station Road,
Milnsbridge.
Hudols.

My Dear Laughing Motorbyke,,
I hope you are having no trouble in aquiring your petrol ration, because should you have to garage your laugh, you would hardly seem the same person, at least to me. As you see by my letterhead, I am back home, putting my shoulder to the wheel, and what a wheel, I sincerely, though regretfully state, it's badly in need of oiling. I have never been so disgusted in my life, at the disgraceful way Hopkinson's Ltd, is managed. We are not welding, we are pushed from pillar to post, and today, after asking the foreman for a job, he said "Just stand there in that corner". That was at 7-45 at the latest, and at 3-15 in the afternoon, I was still standing in my corner. I'm

By the way, this is my second letter to you, but one of the babies chewed it so I had to burn it.[17] I gave you a detailed account of my holiday too, and I'm afraid I haven't the patience or the time to repeat, so you must forgive me.

My holiday was gorgeous, and the place magnificent. I will enclose a letter, or part of a letter to my Mother which will convey just exactly how I felt.[18] I was overwhelmed – absolutely. I never saw my blue-eyed Canadian again, worse luck, but I was more content, and happy with my adorable boy. He really is a darling, and I love him so much. I only hope to God he doesn't have to go overseas, and even if he does, I pray he will come back.

I am very surprised at Amy's appearance. She is so worn and thin, she doesn't drink any more, smoke any more, neither does

---

[17] Possibly her sister Pat's baby.

[18]

Inverary,
Argyllshire,
Scotland

[late July 1942]

|Dear Mother]

. . . and so did it fall before my greedy eyes. Huge mountains [. . .] as the sun caught them. Darker and larger still, looking like dark, solemn sentinels guiding their offspring aloft. I encircled four monstrous lochs and even went round Loch Lomond. Some of them were pleasantly blue, but one or two looked like gigantic pools of ink, splashed with grey where the wind rippled the surface, when suddenly it seemed as if an unseen hand had touched a switch and illuminated a myriad of lights as the sun suddenly burst forth and touched the ripples. It was simply magnificent. Here we are surrounded by mountains and the . . . light in the shore of Loch [Tufide?]. I can paddle every day and we catch mussels and winkles also. When the tide goes out I was paddling and I caught a baby herring. I shall never rest mother until I know that you have seen it. Mr and Mrs Peel are charming and so are all the people I have yet met. Mrs Peel went to Fife for afternoon tea, yesterday. By the way I wished I had brought more clothes. The tea was lovely, really Scotch, with hot buttered scones and scotch cake, really plastered with butter, shortbread and biscuits – hot – and rum! Gosh did I smack my lips you bet I did. Tomorrow Mrs Peel and I are going round the Duke of Argyle's castle and then going to a dance at a camp were I shall have to be vaccinated or I should not be allowed home. On Monday the news came down to Firness that all leave is cancelled even local, so it meant Jack would be unable to come home. I was put out rather . . . There are still cases [of smallpox] being notified. The first night we were here [on Sunday] we all went to a PCO's house |Platoon Commanding Officer] further along the shore, and we all had our supper. I got on with Mr Brown like a house on fire and Mrs Peel told me he is very conservative in his likes and his dislikes. So I was very lucky. It will be a good thing for Jack too if he gets well in with him. He's coming down tonight to tell

she swear. You won't know her. I'm afraid her new romance is getting the better of her.[19] I hope she starts bucking up, she hardly eats anything. Well dear, they are all talking, and I keep joining in the conversation and so lose my train of thought, so I think I will have to close.

I'm very glad the tubes turned out well. I wish I could do some for you right now.[20] I hope you like my little present. Give my best regards to your Father, my love to Walter and Dorothy. I'm sorry my little affair didn't materialise until manners for breakfast. By the way, I have some real good jokes to tell you. A woman was being chased by a huge Bull. A man looking over the hedge shouted, 'what are you running for lady, can't you take it?' 'Of course I can take it, but I can't keep a calf in a council house'!!! I will write the rest in your next letter. Well Goodbye my dear Val, be good, (if you can), and take care of yourself. Remember me to Gottfried (if he is interested).

Please write soon my dear, and cheer this lonely soul in exile. We are all well – all except the firebrand, but soon I think her torch will be relit.[21] Eleanor looks much better.[22] Ethel's mother has

---

me my fortune – I believe he is very good. Mrs Peel and myself are going down the beach again, so I will close this letter now. I only wish that people who suffer from an inferiority complex could come here for a week or two. The magnitude and the glory of nature would soon crack the feeling of 'I'm it'. The mountains and the trees make you feel very very small indeed. In comparison it makes you realise there is [something] bigger than [you] and more mighty. Scotland at least the part where I am fulfils the phrase the glory of God how great is the Lord, and marvellous. Please give my love to Frank and tell him I will bring him some white heather back with me, in fact for you all, I am looking forward to coming back and give you all more verbal accounts of this wonderful spot. The weather is quite good considering we are in the Highland but occasionally a few drops of rain. A regretful journey up but I will tell you all about that later. I have some rations down ready from Lockwood, I should get them. Well I really must go, so goodbye and god bless. Tell Frank to be good. We don't know there is a war on here. Very few [. . .] as there are no electricity or gas, just paraffin lamps for lighting and for cooking so you can imagine how rural it is. I could write and write and write and write. I feel so eloquent but I must close now, so cheerio, hope to see you soon all on Sunday.

Lots of love, Agnes [From the private collection of John Helme]

[19] Possibly this 'new romance' refers to Chick or the older Frank.
[20] It is interesting that Agnes thinks of doing test pieces as something that would please Valentine.
[21] Probably Amy, given what Agnes has said about her earlier in the letter.
[22] See Nellie's letters for details of her illness.

taken her engagement very badly, but she will get over that.[23] Goodnight and God keep you safe. I hear Sheffield was bombed again, please keep clear of danger.[24] I really must go now, so goodbye for the last time.

   Love,
    Agnes

---

[23] Ethel had been engaged previously to a man killed in action. Her engagement to John Kergon was clearly difficult for her mother. See Letter 45.

[24] There were no bombs dropped in Huddersfield or Penistone.

11   *An unwanted pregnancy*

9 Station Road,
Milnsbridge,
Hudds

31 August 1942

My Very Dear Vagrant,
        I need hardly tell you who instigated me, in the term
'Vagrant', but before I begin my letter, let me apologise for using
pencil.[25] You see, I am writing this whilst I am supposed to be
WORKING.
        The dreadfully hard job I have been assigned to do, is as
follows. Jack (the man in charge of the machine) puts on two
reineckers (if you know what they are) and sets a wheel off, which
bores grooves all the way round. Thus: [illustration of wheel] That
procedure takes 40 to 50 mins. My job is to sit smoking, watching
the wheels go round. Lively isn't it!! When one is completed I just
tell Jack, he puts on another, and I resume my vigil for another boring
period. I will tell you how I managed to find this wonderful position.
Referring to my previous letter, I told you how I had given myself
authority to paint. I had been painting ever since, with the exception
of Friday and Saturday, which I didn't come to work, owing to my
neuralgia. Yesterday afternoon, Emily, and Amy, came down for a
chat, and being as there were five of us in one corner, we must have
looked a lot. Anyhow Willie Brook came, the bald headed B-R,
and seeing us came up. 'BLLLLOODY HELL – can't you scatter about
a bit, or else get on with your work.' 'Work?' said I, 'we have none.'
'Oh,' said he, 'I can soon find you a job.' This is the JOB?? After he
had left me I trotted round to Jenny and Ethel, and told them
where I worked. After a few minutes round to me they both came
marching, standing laughing at my hard hob. Also, who came
marching round, but Brooky, stood glowering at the girls, and
bawled, 'BLLLLOODY HELL FIRE, I've brought her round here to
separate you, Bloody get on with your work.' They had no alternative
but to walk back like a couple of ducks, nearly treading on each
other's tails. Talk about laugh!! We nearly split our sides, and all the
men laughed too. Of course, every time we see each other, we say
'Bloody get on with your work'. It's more amusing if you hear him
say it, he sticks at BL for quite a long time before he gets the OODY

[25] Amy?

out. We have just started work again, after having a singsong at (Sheffield) (see where my mind was) Eleanor's. We took three men with us too, we had a real jolly $\frac{1}{2}$ hr. The poor widow woman, kept coming in smiling, but very frail looking.[26]

     I'm glad I went up to Scotland and had such a lovely time. It's a shame it's such an awful long way I can't go so often – hedgebottoming or no hedgebottoming.[27] It's nearly as bad as 'Copper bottoming 'em Mum'. I'm rather surprised at your thinking I am immoral. Imagine a person as beautiful, inspiring, intelligent, and as good, if not absolutely perfect, immoral. Why it's blasphemy. All joking on one side though, I can tell you, I may talk bad, but I certainly am not. Do you know Val, I have a disgusting headache, I think my halo must be too tight.

     You ask me if I mind you taking my letter to show your Mother. I am indeed honoured to think you thought it worthy enough to take to her, but please don't let your Dad read it, he might think me too sentimental, and soft. When is he coming over to Hops? I'm afraid if he doesn't come quickly, he will find me a shadow, worn away with fatigue. Talking of shadows I only weigh 6 stn 7 lbs now.[28] I thought getting married would build me up, but I'm afraid it's knocking the stuffing out of me. Oh! by the way, I have had a rash at the top of my right leg, and I was very worried, as regards smallpox. Anyhow, the nurse told me something had either been spilled, or dropped on it, to irritate it. Now what could it be? I'll give you three guesses, as to what I think it is!

     I am hoping, that what you expected to materialise before 12 months, will be proved a failure.[29] At first I was going to go through with it, had it been true, but yesterday, and Wednesday, I dosed myself with raw gin, so I am hoping I shall have company shortly. I should start tomorrow, but I have no messenger yet. But it may be a bit delayed.[30]

     I am going up to Emily's on Sunday. Amy, and, I'm not sure, but I think Jenny, is too. The time is passing so slowly, it is only 2 o'clock now. If it wasn't for me writing to you, I'm afraid I should be asleep. I wish to goodness I could be filling a tube, right now.

---

[26] Eleanor's mother.

[27] Hedgebottoming is a crack at Valentine's sleeping out under a hedge with her boyfriend one night when they failed to get a room in the village where he was posted.

[28] Given Agnes was quite tall, she was seriously underweight.

[29] A baby.

[30] Gin was supposed to induce a miscarriage.

Is Walter still losing his temper at Dorothy? Please give them my love, and also Edna. Jack sent his love to you in his last letter. You ask me when his next leave is due. I think October. I should simply love some white heather from your garden. I shall cherish it, as I cherish the gifts that came from your fingers, just because they did pass from your fingers. Please don't think me sentimental, because I only stated a true fact. You will never know, really, just how much we do think of you, and your Father. I'm sure had he heard the remarks we were habitually passing, his face, neck and ears would have taken on the hue of an eastern sunset. Well dear I can't think of anything else at the moment, so I will draw to a close, and go and have a word with Ethel. I read Emily's letter today in which you called me Fanny twice! My goodness I'll dust your pants.[31] I will also enclose the typed letter you sent, I must apologise for not sending it before. Well here's cheers to you, and keep out of danger. I'm glad the raids were not bad. So here's to the next time. Goodbye, and God Bless you All.

     Lots of Love,

        Leonora Agnes x

P.S. I hear you may be coming here if more girls come welding.[32] Gee! Will we all have a beano. I hope you come quickly. Fancy me writing all this time. Emily looks ill, Amy a wee bit better. A.

---

[31] Agnes had been given the nickname Fanny Four Rod.

[32] Only one woman came after them to Hopkinsons as a welder, a year later. However she did not stay long. Castle, E. (14 Sept 1995), personal interview, Huddersfield, U of Sussex, Eng.

12 *Women on the sick list*

FROM MRS J. HELME. Know her? I wonder?
9 Station Road,
Milnsbridge,
Hudds

[early September 1942]

My Dear Val,

The time is 2.00 p.m., and I sit here in nightgown, and dressing gown penning you these lines. No! I am not playing truant from work, but I am on the sick list. It all started a week last Wednesday, with a stiff neck, to which I didn't pay very much attention. Thursday evening, whilst washing round my peninsular, I brought my fingers in contact with a lump in the bottom of my hair. I naturally thought it was a swollen gland.

Next morning, I go straight to the ambulance room and report it, and the nurse dressed my lump to my satisfaction. Later in the day, my head began to sting, and when I complained to Ethel, she advised me to go to the nurse again. I did, and found my head all down the left hand side was very sore to touch, and covered in lumps. I was very upset, and the nurse said I must have medical attention at once, so Saturday morning I went to see Dr Smythe, and he threw me straight onto the club. He says my nerves are absolutely worn out, I must have a strong tonic, and complete rest. My neck, throat, head, and ear, are awfully sore. I have had a rash all behind my ear, and up in my hair, and the funny thing is, it is all down one half of my head, my right side is absolutely normal, even the right side of my throat. It's uncanny.

Just one more thing before I finish talking about myself. I am still in the list of 'Expectant Mothers'. I have been taking those famous little black pills nearly all week, but to no effect as yet. I am very upset, but should it really come, it shall be called after you. My mother is most upset.[33]

Thanks for your letter dear, I am so glad you are having a holiday, and your escapades with G always provide me with a real good laugh. You are both such devils, if you will pardon the expression. He seems a most admirable man, full of fun, which to me makes life seem a much more acceptable place in which to live.

---

[33] Agnes's mother was very worried about her daughter's pregnancy because of her fragile health.

It is a true quotation of Ella Wheeler Wilcox's: 'Laugh, and the world laughs with you, weep, and you weep alone'. You certainly see a lot of fun in life, keep it up lass. Are you staying at Ilkeston? Why not go to Lowestoft or Gurlston, but I suppose it is a restricted area. I can just imagine the episode of the purse and trunk, and the smiling bravado with which you would face the situation.

I miss the girls very much, I feel so lonely at home, I miss Jack more than ever, now. I am in the 'longing' phase. All I want are chips, boiled potatoes with butter on, and fruit. I'm going crazy for some fruit. I've even begged a bottle of concentrated orange juice from Pat. Oh I forgot to tell you I told the doctor I suspected I was pregnant, (it is six weeks today since my last show) and he doesn't take it seriously he seems to think I am delayed as a complication of my illness. He also thought I was sickening for Chicken Pox of all things.

Well dear, I'm afraid I must close now, my pains in my ear and head are becoming too bad. Please give my regards to your lucky parents, (if they have finished knocking the shipyards about).

You have heard me speak of Clem down at Devonport, well he is up in Inveraray with Jack.[34] I am so pleased.

Yes it is quite true about my bed sitting room. If I may, I will offer it for your convenience whilst you are residing at Hudds. Well dear Val I really must close now, don't forget to drop me a line, your letters are such a tonic.

Good afternoon and look after yourself. I should love to see you whilst I am on the club. Love to Dot, Edna, and Walter. I suppose he has entirely forgotten me by now. How's Ferdinand?

It has just occurred to me I didn't sign my letter so here I add a few more lines. By Ferdinand I of course referred to B_LL.[35]

Our Tom sailed for the Middle East this week. He was marvellous, I should love you to have met him. He was wonderful. Oh! how about a nice little oblong of paper with your likeness on one side. Savee?[36]

Good Luck

God Bless

Agnes

---

[34] Jack had been posted in Devonport before Inveraray. Clem was one of his colleagues.
[35] Ferdinand is John Bull, the bully at Welding Rods.
[36] Tom was her brother. She is asking for a photo of Valentine.

13   *'My Dear Instigator of Laughs'*

9 Station Road,
Milnsbridge,
Hudds

[c. 8 September 1942]

My Dear Instigator of Laughs,
I laughed until I cried when I read your last description of the latest adventure, of the hero, and heroine of our most important love story. I wonder what the next breathtaking incident will be in the next instalment? I can just imagine G[37] swinging like Tarzan suspended in mid air, only by his teeth, and then gracefully drifting to a grassy mound and gently lowering himself by the side of a woman – very brown, and very bare, munching nuts, (cocoa nuts) or were they prunes, from under an electric saw?
Seriously though! Whatever will you be doing next? The incident of your camping out amused me tremendously. It would have just been your luck had the peering gentleman turned out to be a homeguard, and accused you of being a fifth columnist.[38]
Dear Val, I am awfully sorry about my book, but your letter did not arrive until Friday morning, and I thought it was too late then. If you write back return of post I can forward it on this week, or let me know for Thursday. Or if you liked to save time I could get your ticket from Hudds, but you would have to register your envelope, to be safe. I would willingly buy it for you, you know that, but my pocket, with not working just now is a little thin, and to put the top hat on, I have a pound or two to put down on Saturday. I am really saying goodbye to my molars. They are a sight Val, my front one has broken away still further. I'm frightened but I shall be glad to be rid.
Please think about my falling asleep at 3 o'clock, I am having Eripan (needle in my arm) and having all of them out. I don't know what time I'm expected out of my 'doze', but I have to have someone call for me at 4 o'clock, and then they will find me resting. If I don't waken would you grant me a favour, and still send me that white heather??

---

[37] Gottfried.
[38] Another hedgebottoming episode? If Valentine and Gottfried had been spotted by a Home Guard, they might have been grilled, as Gottfried's Germanic accent had already caused him to be arrested as a potential spy at least once.

I'm afraid Grandma is still on holiday – she hasn't come home yet.[39] It is 2 months this week. My breasts are very, very painful, and at night they ache. I have been to Doctor Smythe tonight. Did I tell you it is a nerve up the left side of my neck and head that has shattered, so he is trying to feed it, through feeding myself. I am decidedly improved but my head is painfully sore, the lumps are still there, and the spots. I hate going to bed – I can only lay in one position because of my head and breasts. Jack is begging of me every letter to go to Scotland to recuperate, and I told the doctor tonight. He said 'by all means the change of air would work wonders. My God what with a sore head, lumps, teeth out, anticipated journeys, and er, and little bits o' things, you really are in a way.' I blushed and answered, 'Yes! but of all the complaints you have mentioned, the "little bits o' things" I don't want that to go any further.' He laughed and put his arm around my shoulders and told me I mustn't worry, all that happens is an act of God. That's twice he has told me that. I suppose, and rightly so, you will be tired of hearing my complaints.

I have been most unfortunate this week. Eleanor has been to see me twice, and each time I have been at Pat's. Last Saturday night, Amy went to where Frank plays, with a gentleman, I was so disappointed I didn't go, I nearly did, because according to Dr's orders I must prove myself a living proof of 'Guinness is good for you'. Anyhow she is coming down on Wednesday. I am so pleased. I have started enjoying myself slightly now, but if I go to the movies, I have to go in the afternoon, with being on the Club. How I wish I could be like you. I wish your health and vitality were contagious. I should really then be well.

Looking at your letter again, I sincerely hope G did not take cold, when his nether regions were exposed to Winter's cruel blast.

Speaking of your undesirable companion, I once suffered much the same sort of experience coming from Manchester to Penistone. He actually did pounce – in Woodhead tunnel, but my teeth served me well again. Jack will be crowing when my fang does the disappearing trick. I feel I could sit and write and write and better write, just as I loved to stand and talk to you, but although I have not told you all I should have liked, I really must make my Allenbury's Food, (builds bonny babies) and go to bed, it is very, very late. Goodnight, God bless you and all your relatives and G.

Love Agnes

Love to Dorothy and Walter, the cynical cynic, and hope to see you soon, Agnes.

[39] Her period.

14   A visit to the dentist

9 Station Road,
Milnsbridge,
Huddersfield

[mid-September 1942]

My Dear Sweet Val,
        Yes it really is me, I really came out of the worst nightmare
I ever had, worse luck, I almost wish I hadn't. That is why I asked
you to send the white heather, for if I didn't come out. Please don't
think I deliberately asked for it, but it is beautiful, and so fragrant.
It is on the wall of our sitting room, just as you sent it. Thanks a
lot, I shall always keep it. It arrived Saturday morning, so it seemed
an emblem of good luck. Unluckily, I have to undergo the
eaneasthetic (that's not right) again, as under Dr's orders I wasn't
allowed to have them all extracted. I had to go at 2.30, to take a
little capsule, which made me feel tired, and at 3 pm I took the chair.
When I came out, I had to have my gums sewn up, so I shouldn't
lose any blood. It was agony – worse than having my teeth out, I
nearly fade away now, when I think of my next dose. I do look a
bonny B-R now. I have two huge fangs at the front, just like an
ape's. [Illustration of her fangs.] Anyway, I'm not dead yet, but I
wish Jack was with me, I should not feel so terrified.
        Just before I conclude all my wailings I must tell you Dr
Smyth told me last night again, that I am pregnant. It isn't my fault,
my dear, I took those capsules for a fortnight, but to no effect. I'm
getting resigned to the situation now, but to tell you candidly Val,
it wouldn't take much for me to throw myself in front of a bus. I
get desperate at times. I have had Amy with me all weekend, bless
her. I don't know what I should have done. She put new life into
me. She was mostly in company of a gentleman, by the name of
Frank, a slightly older man, but very nice and most generous. He
was buying drinks for Amy, my mother, my Frank, another Agnes,
himself, and myself. Rums and whiskies were the order of the day.
You missed a treat dear.
        By the way when are you coming? I hope it is soon. When
Amy comes to see you, I shall probably come too. You ask about
my not being at Moldgreen. I hardly like leaving home while I am
better, but don't you worry. Mabel, (my friend), will see you alright.
I am longing to see you again. Give my kind regards to G. your
Dad and Mam, Dorothy, and Walter. Was that your home address

on your last letter 'Crowsnest'? Goodbye, and God Bless you, and keep you safe. Jack may be home in two weeks.
Goodbye.
Love
Agnes

P.S. Keep news of Amy, and Frank between we three, as he works at Hops. We three seem to be real conspirators, don't we?
Agnes

15 A confession

9 Station Road,
Milnsbridge,
Hudds

[Early October 1942]

My Dear Val,

Many, many thanks for your first instalment of my life's history. I was so pleased to receive your letter, I was so afraid I had offended you in some way, with you not writing. I wrote a letter to you, but I burned it. (Should that word have been burnt?). Your letters do me good, and believe me, I need doing good right now. I have never before laboured under a guilty conscience, or been so utterly miserable as I am now. I am the sorry victim of circumstances. I will assume the pose of a confessor, and you become the Father of Mercy. I will start at the beginning.

Last week I was so upset, as Jack was being drafted, and I hadn't heard for a week, which from Jack, as you know, is a long time. I had been staying at his mother's, and on the Friday, Elsie, and I, arranged to go out. (She lives next door to Jack.) Just prior to our going, a letter came for his mother, saying he was on the 'Viceroy of India'. I was pleased to know where he was, and knowing there would be a letter for me at home, I promised Mam Helme, I would go straight home, to collect same.

Elsie and I went to Town, and decided to make a day of it, and go to a Cafe for tea. We did, from there going to the first house of the Palace. It was only 7.25 when we came out, so as I had promised to go up to the 'White Lion' for Frank and Betty, I told Elsie I would go with her for an hour to the 'Spinner's Arms', and then leave her to go to Lockwood. Arriving at the Spinner's, we were quickly surrounded, with soldiers, and three commercial travellers came [through], and they kept coming. I was drinking Sovereign Ales and my head felt like a great big pumpkin. I felt awful. Elsie said 'come and sleep with me my dear'. It was only about 50 yards away from her door. I was puzzled, because I darn't let Jack's Mother see me as I was, because she doesn't like us taking a drink, and I knew if she somehow got to know I had stayed at Elsie's all night without calling there, I should be in greater disgrace. So we decided to say I had never been at Elsie's, but had gone home to Mabel's at Moldgreen. As you will have gathered, I hadn't been home for my expected letter. Elsie and I had just had supper, when there came a knock upon the door. It turned out to be two of the soldiers, that had been with us all night. Johnnie, and another Jack. Well to cut a long story short, we talked until it was too late for them to go home. We all retired, not getting undressed or anything like that, but we were four in a bed. About 2.30 Elsie was knocked up, and a voice inquired 'Was Agnes there?' Of course, owing to our circumstances, she said 'No!' Then she said, 'God Agnes, its your Jack.' I nearly died, but I couldn't do anything, only torture myself with thinking he was just through the wall. I intended rising early, rushing home for my letters and coming straight back, to prevent his searching for me. I did just as I had planned, put a very good act on at home and rushed back, to find Jack and his Father had already gone. Elsie in the meantime had told them I had been at Mabel's. I nearly collapsed when Mam Helme told me Mabel's was the first port of all, so I had to concoct yet another lie. I told Mam Helme I had slept out all night. I was so low with lying all round, and yet being found out in another huge lie, and on the top of that, when I knew he had only come for 48 hrs, and I thought of all those precious hours I had jeopardised, I rushed out, to fling myself under a trolleybus, but Mam Helme tore my fur coat, pulling me back. I felt absolutely wretched, in fact I am now. He came back about dinner time loaded with flowers for me, and he nearly ate me, and I him. I've never known before just how much he really means to me. He went back Sunday evening, and apart from a telegram on Monday, I have had no further word from him. There is only one conclusion to draw, he has sailed. God knows where he is, or when I shall hear from him. I feel smaller than a microbe, and I'm so miserable, I do nothing but cry all day. If he had come on his ten days, I shouldn't feel so bad, but to think he has gone, it nearly drives me insane.

Monday to try and forget, I went to the Ritz with Jean, and just imagine my horror, when 'Mrs Jack Helme is wanted immediately at the box office', flashed onto the screen. I thought Jack's train had crashed or something, but Mother soon put my fears at rest. Ron, and Gordon, are sailing in a fortnight to Africa, and they came to say goodbye.[40] He also told me I should have married an airman instead of a sailor, that he knew now what a B-Y fool he had been, how he really and truly had missed his boat. I pretended to be puzzled, and asked what he meant. He said he wouldn't tell me, it would give me something to think about whilst he's gone.

---

[40] Ron was a partner in Agnes's singing performances. He had a stage personality that was also a kind of naughty 'double' identity, called Gordon. He seemed to have expressed romantic feelings for Agnes just as he was posted.

He's going to write. I hope they come back. Well my dear, you will be tired of all my troubles, but it does me good to get them out of my system. Mother sends her love, she thinks you are a lovely woman. Congratulations my dear. Fan too sends all the best. He's a great guy. Give my regards to your Dad, and Mam, and Gottfried.

I was so happy seeing you, thanks a million for being so kind to me. I had a damn good laugh at your interpretation of myself, and above all, the likeness, as well as the skit at my cobbling. You really ought to be a cartoonist. Try doing yourself, Bull, and Walter.

Well my dear it is teatime, and Frank is due any minute.[41] I'm still losing weight. I weigh 6 stn 5½ lbs, now. Last night I joined the paratroops, the wind lifted me completely up, and had it not been for a soldier who very obligingly was in the way of my so-called flight, I might have landed in Coleridge Rd. I really thought my umbrella would have been inside out. He insisted he saw me home, to keep my feet on the ground. Outside our door he kissed me, and etc., but I wasn't having any. He kept murmuring 'Gorgeous', in my ear, and I thought, 'It's a damn good job it's blackout, if he only saw my fangs.' Anyhow I managed to get away saying I had my husband's and my chips, and they were going cold. Fan does come in handy sometimes. Mother remarked about my hat being on one side, so I told them what had happened. We all had a good laugh.

Goodbye and God keep you safe,
Love Agnes

P.S. I should really have said God keep you good, shouldn't I? Write soon. Lots of Love Agnes.

P.P.S. Its a good job this letter won't be censored, or they might draw the conclusion I am a thoroughly bad woman, habitually sleeping with strange men, bumping into Soldiers, having a man in the house to whom I refer as husband, and on top of that, two airmen who caused a commotion just to see me, and one of them practically telling me he loves me. What a bad, wicked woman I must be. I forgot to tell you on arrival at Hudds at 11.45 Friday night, Jack walked to my home first collecting my mail, and then back again down to Leeds Rd., and after all that he was up at 6.45 getting ready to look for me, and went without his breakfast. Poor Devil. He must love me. Bless him.

---

[41] Frank Helme, her father-in-law, was a good friend.

16   *A nightingale sang*

9 Station Road,
Milnsbridge,
Hudds

[22 October 1942]

My Dear Val,
        No! I've not been residing at the bottom of a river again,
but at Penistone for a week. You nearly had two visitors on Tuesday,
as Edna had to bring Yvonne to be operated upon, and she intended
coming to see you, whilst Yvonne was being done, but she couldn't
manage it. I was coming also but I should have to have brought the
baby, so I thought it was too much.[42] I was so disappointed Edna
didn't see you though, and so was she. She did like you so much
the last time you met. You should be very swelled headed, at the
compliments my humble family bestows upon you. Pat, Frank,
Mam, Edna, and last, but not least, myself. I'm not in the habit of
paying compliments, nor do I like receiving them (in spite of my
dumb expression, as you claim) but I don't think you can possibly
conceive how much real pleasure and how honoured I feel to have
your friendship. Please don't think I'm offering you strawberries and
cream on a silver platter, or that I am paving the way to borrow
something or other, I am merely stating a fact.
        I still cannot write to Jack. He is doing something, as he is
suffering from sea sickness, and his envelopes (when he writes) are
marked 'On Active Service', and 'From His Majesty's Ships'. He
often mentions you. There was a grand Ball on Friday at Penistone
you ought to have been able to go with me. I didn't go, I was short
of a partner. There are hundreds of black Americans in Penistone
– yes – I was fascinated to death, but I'm still living. I was in
conversation with one Monday. I was returning to Edna's from the
chip shop, and I was whistling, 'Skylark'. As I turned up the Avenue
a very deep voice said, 'Hm, Hm, a nightingale sang in Berkeley
Square'. I was very surprised, and looked all around, to ascertain if
I was the one being spoken to, and then I noticed he was black. I
thought my heart was breaking its strings, it pulled so hard. I
controlled myself, and said cheekily, 'Perhaps, but you have hold
of the wrong bird, but there is a moon'.

---

[42] This was probably her sister Pat's baby.

I then took to my heels, and ran as if my very life depended on it, and his laughter followed me all the way home. I was really frightened for if he should follow, as he stood about 6ft 5ins. A real 'Paul Robeson type'.

I should have had the rest of my teeth out today at 2.45, but Grandma came yesterday Oct 21st, so it has been postponed yet again.[43] I do get fed up. I wish they were out. It will probably be next Thursday or Saturday week now, how about coming over to hold my hand? I might be brave then.

How is God? your God I mean. Any more adventures? I hope he is well, and the man who made a meal of worms is quite OK. Rather a good idea, what!! French people eat slugs, and snails, why not patent a new worm soup? Goody, goody.

Fan thanks you for your compliment to his Sonata, and says he would like to have a night out. With you of course. (Inevitable). Kathleen has started proceedings this week. I hope he gets free, he's too grand a lad to be tied as he is. I should love to come to Sheffield if only to try my hand at welding. I'm afraid I shall have to be trained all over again, and would I be glad if it was so. How is your Dad? Give him my kind regards and your Mam also. Remember me to Dot. I nearly was sent to jail for failing to register for firewatching in spite of being under the doctor. How did you go on? Your last letter said you were considering being a conscientious objector.[44] I hope you are within the law in that too. Well dear, I have written four letters today, and I must get ready to go to the doctor's. Our Tom has landed in South Africa. I have written to Mr and Mrs Holmes today too. Well my hedgebottom vagrant, I must write 'Finish', to this scribble, hoping you are well, and not down hearted. (Imagine that – I can't). Cheerio, and lots of Luck to you, and God. I saw Mrs Miniver last night.[45] It's good. I did enjoy it.

Goodbye and God Bless You Always.

Love Agnes xxx

your meek little rat

---

[43] Her period. She had miscarried some while before.

[44] This was more than likely a joke on Valentine's part.

[45] *Mrs Miniver* was the famous Hollywood version of Jan Struther's column in *The Times* about the daily life of an upper-middle-class English woman. Starring Greer Garson, it was taken as the epitome of British civilian resistance, 'smiling through'.

17   *Absolutely fed up with everything*

9 Station Road,
Milnsbridge,
Hudds

[October/November 1942]

My Dear Val,
Please accept my profound apologies, for failing to write
ere this, but after I returned from Penistone, I stayed at my Mother-
in-Law's, for almost a fortnight, so I couldn't very well answer. I
returned home to have the last of my teeth extracted, but Mr Palmer
said I was like a mad woman in the chair. It was Hell. I felt everything,
and to make matters worse, I have still got my fangs. It made me
quite ill again this weekend, the Dr has put me on the Club for another
month, and now the Dentist told me this morning not one out of
ten men would have attempted my teeth in my condition. I was
quite upset, when he said I was a reputation-wrecker, because other
people couldn't understand why I had to go so many times. It was
his idea, I wanted the lot out at one dose, as well you know. I think
it was a nasty thing to say. I am keeping my fangs and I have to go
the second week in December, to see if I am ready to be modelled.
I just feel absolutely fed up with everything.
I haven't seen, or heard anything of Amy for a long while,
but last Saturday night she went to the White Lion, and of course
I wouldn't be there. I have gone week after week – just to see her,
and the very first time, I'm not there, she comes. She told Fan, she
would come down Sunday, and we waited, and waited, but no Amy.
I still don't know where Jack is. It's dreadful not having
letters, I do wish to God he'd come home. I feel utterly dejected.
Our Tom has landed in East London, S. Africa. I am just
writing to him, sending airgraph, letter and card. I have just completed
Tom's correspondence so I will carry on. Thanks dear, for budget.
How ever you have patience to write all that, I don't know. Will
you ever keep your little nose out of scrapes? I wonder. What does
God think of you, and your adventures.[46] Speaking of God, I was
dreaming of him last night.
I will enclose a letter I had from Ron. Tell me what you
think. Is he pulling my leg as regards his liking me, or is he sincere?
He's such an idiot, I can't imagine him really serious.

[46] Gottfried.

I have no news lass, life is very drab just now. I may be coming to Sheffield next week. I've written to Mrs Holmes about a pair of shoes I left to be repaired, and asked her to forward them. It is nearly two weeks since I wrote my second letter, and still there is no reply. What do you think? I'm beginning to consider you my information bureau, or my Brain's Trust. Mam, and Fan both send best love to you. All my best wishes to your Mam, and Dad. By the way my machine is at last ready for me. I do want to go back to work. Love to you in haste, Agnes.

God Bless You, and keep out of danger (of any description). If possible remember me to G.

Agnes

18   *Pepper Pot Agnes*

9 Station Road,
Milnsbridge,
Hudds

[October/November 1942]

My Dear Val,
Please excuse brevity, but I have just remembered you
want the enclosed, so I will send you a newsy letter later. Goodbye
and God Bless you all.
So bye bye for now
Love
Agnes

Glad Amy came Monday. She had her arm in a sling when I saw
her. Her new romance getting a little too hot??? I wonder.
Love Agnes

same.

Dear Val,
I'm in a deuced of a hurry so please my dear, excuse me. I
was away last week when your letter arrived, down at Leeds Road.
Edna was coming Tues. Did she come? Cheers Val, I'm starting work
on Monday, I should have started today, but Mam is far from well,
more details later. We are busy these days Pat, and I, we have so
many engagements.[47] (Soldiers of course.) Love to your Dad, Mam,
God, and a goodly portion yourself.
God Bless You Love
PTO xx Agnes xx

How about coming over, and putting my weary nerves at rest? I
shall be absolutely terrified until I get to know the boss. Ask your
Dad, for compassionate leave.

I'm hoping to see Amy tomorrow night. I do hope so, I really do
think a lot about her. Isn't my writing enviable? I can hardly read
it myself. Good Luck to you.

I still have no word from Jack. I feel positively ill sometimes. Cheerio
Pepper Pot Agnes.

[47] Pat and Agnes sang together as 'The Green Sisters'.

19 *Your most welcome letter*

9 Station Road,
Milnsbridge,
Hudds

[October/November 1942]

My Dear Val,
Many thanks for your most welcome letter, I nearly jumped out of bed, with joy, when Mam, brought me your letter. I will certainly meet you at approx. 6.30 at the Queen's Hotel. I do hope you are comfortable there. This afternoon I received a letter from Amy telling me the glad news, and the disconcerting news of Jenny.[48] I really think she was too headstrong. Amy is coming back from Ilkley on Monday night, so she may meet us. I am seeing her Friday. Would you care if Frank (mine) came, or would you think it presumptuous of me? He would love to meet you, and Monday is not the only time you are to be in the company of the terrible twins – according to Amy's letter.[49] Anyhow, all the news when I see you.
Love to all at Sheffield.
Yours in Haste
Love,
Agnes

P.S. Amy's description is very true to life as you will see by my preceding letter. Mother is looking forward to seeing you too. Regards to your Dad, and God. Agnes

[48] Jenny had been dismissed from Hopkinsons for being 'rude' to the manager. The other women thought she had probably sought dismissal because she didn't like the job.
[49] The terrible twins are Amy and Emily.

III   Welding a Friendship: Letters from Amy Brooke, 'The Mighty Atom'

Amy Brooke (later Hargate) was born in 1914, in Huddersfield. She was one of five children, Harold, Frank, Evelyn, Amy and Hilda. Harold and Hilda were teachers, Frank was an engineer and Evelyn had a family. Harold was notable for his fine embroidery and cooking skills. Her father was a mechanic and chauffeur for a local mill boss; her mother didn't do any paid work because of ill health. At 14, Amy left school to work in the mill. She was called up for training as a welder at age 28.

20   Beginning work

15 Chestnut Street,
Sheepridge,
Huddersfield

6 July 1942

Dear Miss Pearson,
      Just a line to let you know how we are getting along. We have been sitting up and taking notice today, but tomorrow, all being well we shall be on the job. Mr Charlesworth is setting the machine for us tonight. We had rather a striking episode at lunch time. All the seats in the Canteen were reserved by different girls so Emily and I ended up outside, and sat on the floor to have our dinner. If we manage alright with the machine this week, we are expected to go on nights next Monday, so just say a prayer for us tomorrow, will you please.
      Emily and I went straight up to see Nellie after we had rung you up, and I regret to say she is ill in bed, but we had not time to go upstairs to see her. As you know it was 12.50 when we left the phone box, so we are going up again tomorrow.
      Well how about my friends in Sheffield? I expect they will have had a nice quiet day.[50] I hope Enid is being looked after. Just tell her they call one of the men working with us Ned, and it reminds me of her when I hear his name. I will be thinking of you all tomorrow when Fanny arrives. She will soon set the ball rolling.

---

[50] Amy and Emily had been sent back three weeks before the rest of the team, who were still in Sheffield (although Nellie was at home because she was ill, here).

It has just dawned on me, it was our night out together tonight was not it? I am sorry I cannot carry out what I had intended to do, but when you come over here I will make up for it with you, (honest to god).

I am feeling very lonely, I do wish I could have stayed with you for another week. I am sat writing to you, but when I have finished this letter I am off for a Cuddly woodle, so it will not be so bad. Evelyn has gone home again. She is expecting Alec for another six days. I am head cook and bottle-washer now, because Mam and Dad are away. There is only Hilda, Harold and yours truly at home, so you will see how busy I am.

I am looking forward to seeing you in Huddersfield very much, but I am afraid it will be a couple of months yet. We are both keeping our ears open, but have not got to know too much as yet. I have not seen Mr Wright yet but we saw Lady Marflit first thing this morning, and she has been in to have a look at us. But she did not gain much.

Emily and I go to Ilkley a week on Saturday, and some Monday after, in August we shall be visiting you for the day. So if you are having a Holiday in August just let us know and then we shall not have a waste[d] trail because we shall have to report back at Hopkinsons for 9.00 o'clock in any case.

Thank you very much for sending my mail on. It was very nice of you. Please don't forget to send me a snapshot of yourself because I want something to look at to remind me of My Happy Days spent in your company. I will draw to a close now because I want to catch this evening's post I will write you on Saturday and let you know how we are doing.

Cheerio and all the Best
Yours very sincerely
Amy

P.S. Cannot send you any sweets on because Mrs Feather has not sent us any yet but we are living in anticipation.[51] Goodnight and Godbless you.

---

[51] The owner of the sweetshop in Sheffield which they used to visit.

21 'I am fair dying to see you again'

15 Chestnut Street,
Sheepridge,
Huddersfield

Sunday [July 1942]

Dear Little Glamour Girl Hearthrob No. 1.

Hello little prairie flower. How have you enjoyed your week end, 'have you had it'? I have had a quiet week end and it is only 10.00 o'clock and I am ready for bed, also all set for morning. I have been at Frank's this evening with my mother and father. They have just come back from Ilkley after a very enjoyable week. Harold was preaching at Wiggan Lane Flower Service this afternoon, and I had forgotten so I rung Emily up and asked her if she would go with me to Chapel. Anyhow she turned up and believe me, what a finger she has got. Septic in it and it is swollen up shocking. But she will be at work tomorrow, whether she works or not, because we have had no wage this week and we are relying on next week's wage for our holidays. We are going up to see Nellie again tomorrow lunch time, so if we hear anything different we will give you a ring. I hope you can manage the five Welding Wonders OK without assistance.[52] I hope they have a lunch time on the beer with you before they leave next Friday, but believe me, they are not coming back to Weld, because I dare gamble the plant will not be ready this month. But with a bit of strategy it may be ready next month. I thank you very much for your kindness to Enid since I came home. She told me on Friday that, had it not been for you and Jenny, she would have been very miserable. So please keep it up this next week for her sake.

They have been putting a new device on our machine this week and we have done very little work since Wed morning. But we shall be cracking in tomorrow because they promised to have it ready for Saturday teatime. The boss told the men off for being so long in doing the job. He said they had spoilt two good girls for him because we were fair getting on well and he knows we were fed up of doing nothing. One snag my dear, we are splitting. One of us has to go on nights after the holidays and the other on days. So that kind of buggers the contract. Eddie and Emily will be working together and Edwin and me. If you hear of any more births

[52] Agnes, Emily, Enid, Ethel, Alice.

in the Lav – please study because you never know what will happen now my guide is leaving me.[53] I shall come to Sheffield the first Monday I am on nights. This will be either a month or five weeks' time and I feel you will not be in Huddersfield before then so we will make it a date. I am fair dying to see you again believe me, my night duty cannot come too soon. But I will let you know later. You will get a letter from the two of us at Ilkley next week, so please look out for a hot one. We are working from 7.30 until 7.00 pm this next week and lucky to know we break up next Friday night or else it would have been from 7.30 am until 4.30 on Saturday. I shall be like a shadow next time we meet. I have to get up at 6.30 on a morning now. My word, it takes some getting into after my holiday in Sheffield. I did not get up until 11.00 today and I had hardly any dinner and no breakfast. I have got back to my old ways again, living on fresh air. My mother is going mad over me because I have just refused my supper.

Well the ring does not appeal to me at all. I don't know what you think about it. It strikes me she has been romancing again. I don't know whatever John carries on for her like he does. I did not see my lover on Friday because I had to see our Frank and also go up to Enid's. Tell Enid I am going up with a joint on Friday so she must keep it dark.[54] I hope you are in the pink and please give the girls my love, also accept the same yourself, and keep smiling. I will write you again on Tuesday. Goodnight and Godbless you.

All The Best,
Yours Very Sincerely
Amyeeeeee

[53] Emily.
[54] Probably a Joint Forces Soldier.

22   'Being alone amongst all the men'

15 Chestnut Street,
Sheepridge,
Huddersfield

Wed[nesday July 1942]

My Dear Little Hedgehog,
          Thank you very much for your most welcome letter. I
thought somehow I should get a letter today, but there were three
waiting for me. Glad to hear you are sorry about us being separated,
but it will not make any difference to the war effort because we have
worked very hard this week. We cut five plates each in turns, as
there are only two machines and one of the men is away poorly, so
Emily and I join.[55] We cut seventy plates out on Monday, eighty
plates yesterday and ninety five today so there will be plenty ready
for Welding when the plant is ready (?). I am very upset about being
alone amongst all the men. but I shall have to face it I expect. It
would not be so bad if there were some more girls in the room.
One of the Welders at Hops put a weld on our new device and what
a slag-hole. I said 'My words, if Mr Pearson saw us do a weld like
that we should be sacked!'
          I am very pleased to hear you are making good use of the
girls before they leave you. 'Have you been out with them for a
farewell do?' Good old Aggie getting her hand in, but it is as well
she is learning how to wash things for a start, because she might be
busy washing Nappies if things don't turn out for the better. I hope
her Sweetheart gets some digs for her, and then maybe her [she]
will be able to finish the job off right, and bring forth fruits.
          Talking about fruit, I have just had some prunes for my sweet
tonight and I was reading your letter at the same time, and did I
laugh. I think mine would be much sweeter than yours, because the
day I wet myself, with laughing, I had some prunes up my knickers
slop, and I threw them under the saw somewhere, but I am in good
condition so you will not be poisoned.[56] Poor Mrs Feather, we think
about her quite often, especially when we are thirsty because we
can only get water. But I don't fancy it these days. Emily says if I

---

[55] They were using an electric saw to cut metal plates because the welding
    machines were not yet ready.
[56] Amy apparently wet her knickers with laughing and threw them under the
    electric saw.

want a drink at Ilkley, I shall have to go alone, so it looks as though I shall have to be teetotal because I dare not go alone.

I am glad to hear Jenny has turned up. I have just had a letter from her. About the ring, I am disgusted with Ethel. I think if she goes away with him and then carries on as before, she is a downright rotter, and like you, I think the sooner she gets Mrs Shaw crossed off and the better.[57]

Yes, I realise I was a naughty thing five timing. But I am one timing now, and strange to say I have to meet my one and only tomorrow night. Oh boy will I love him, you bet I will. I wish it was tonight because I am in the mood, but not to be loved properly. He would never do such a thing as go with another, because he thinks too much about me and if he ever gets in any girl's company, he always tells me, and that only one interests him, that is me. He wrote and asked me to see him at 7.00 pm. Is not it a good job I am not working over, I would have knocked [off] though, I would leave home for him I love him that much. I do wish the war was over.

Glad to hear you had a good weekend but sorry you had to sleep under a hedge. You would not be able to have it? I bet it was cold. I dare not have done it. I don't like sleeping on rugs, but I had to do once. How lovely having a swim alone. I do hope nobody saw you though, but if you had taken a shave like Aggie they would not have known what it was.[58] I have had a letter from Alice, I expect she will be lonely without Nellie. By the way we have been up to Nellie's every dinnertime and she is pleased to see us always, she says she will miss us going. I hope you are looking after Enid for me, I guess she is longing for Saturday. Emily's finger is much better today thank you.

My dear friend, I thank you very much for giving me my name.[59] I often wonder what I am, but I know now. Yes I will give Nellie her letter with the greatest of pleasure. You can rest assured that I will be only too pleased to grant you a favour anytime, believe me you cannot ask too much, (for me), so please bear that in mind. She keeps wanting me to lay on the bed beside her, but I have refused, but tomorrow I will get in, and press your note into her bosom.[60]

I shall be over in three weeks' time. You see I shall be on days after the holiday I think, so that means I will not have a

---

[57] Mrs Shaw was possibly the mother of Ethel's previous fiancé, who was killed in action.

[58] Possibly, Agnes had been shaved, due to the rash on her leg that she writes of. Alternatively this could be an idiomatic phrase.

[59] Possibly a nickname.

[60] See Letter 47.

Monday for a month. So please wait for it, and keep it dark, it's a black pudding, and I want to come alone.[61] But I will write you when I am coming definitely. I shall have to have a short sleep in your Office though in the afternoon, because I shall go to work at 9.00 pm. I will now close, trusting you are in the Pink and feeling none the worse for sleeping out and also after Spring-Cleaning.

     Goodnight and Godbless
          Yours Very Sincerely
               Amyeeeeeeee With Love

[61] A black pudding is local dialect for a secret.

23   Permission to use Valentine's first name

Hudd

10 p.m., Sunday [July 1942]

Dear Miss Pearson,

Thank you very much for your letter to hand on Friday, I thought there would be a reason for you not answering me so soon. I am writing you tonight on a very important matter though. Would you mind forwarding Emily's and my full insurance cards please, because there will be some trouble over them with my sick lodge. You see they ought to have been in no later than July 18th. Alice said that Audrey gave them theirs, and our two were amongst them. But she gave them Audrey back and told her we had left, so she said they would send them on, but we have not got them yet.[62] Emily and I played hell with them for not bringing them, especially when we have looked after them so well. One would have thought they would have used a bit of tact and brought them, because they were due in when they got theirs, anyhow you will do your best no doubt.

Well I am having a hectic time writing this letter my feet are sending me silly with itching. I hope to goodness I am not going to be like Nellie because it's similar you know. I have quite a number of burns on both feet and they itch like bleeding hell when they get warm.

We are all going to Nellie's tomorrow night but of course the VOLUNTEERS are buggered once again. My hours next week are 7.30 a.m. until 7.00 p.m. and Saturday 7.30 a.m. until 4.30 p.m. What do you think about that? The others are stocktaking and finish at 5.00 p.m. and 12.00 a.m. Saturday. Are not they lucky people? Emily is on nights 9.00 p.m. until 7.30 a.m. for a fortnight and then me.

I knew you would be feeling lonely without the mob, but believe me we would have been home this week in any case now the raids have started again, we should not have stopped there. What do you mean when you say 'watch Emily'? She plays hell over you saying that. Yes she has heard from Norman twice since she came home.

Well, I have had a real card from Fanny. It's a fairy on the front and she says, don't I think it is like her. You'll have an idea what I think about it. Had it been the devil I would have said definitely it was like her. She will be at Hops tomorrow, I suppose. There has

[62] Audrey worked at Welding Rods.

been a bit more trouble. The other girls are jealous of us, because
Mother Marflit says we six have to have our dinners in the Staff
Canteen. Are not we lucky? I guess we shall have to make up to
Hops for it, though, when the welding plant is ready. I wish I was
with you welding tomorrow. Honest, I am scared stiff working alone.
Tomorrow I shall miss Emily because we have been together all along.
Believe me, I could murder Arthur for splitting us.

I will have to draw to a close now love, as time is getting
on, but I must say one thing. I thank you very much for giving me
permission to use your Christian name, but under circumstances I
regret I could not, I would sooner give up writing to you altogether.
Thank you all the same.

Cheerio
Goodnight and Godbless,
Yours Sincerely,
Amy with Love

24 A man in the Royal Air Force

15 Chestnut Street,
Sheepridge,
Hudd

26 July 1942

Dear Miss Pearson,

Just a line to let you know I have had a lovely holiday, but I have been kept rather busy, being that it was my cousin's boarding house where I was staying, so I had to give her a helping hand. I have had a right good week and feel ready for work tomorrow. You would enjoy Ilkley very much. Believe me, it's ideal for courting couples, fields, woods, and moors whichever way you walk, and a marvellous swimming pool.

My sisters spent the weekend with us last Saturday, and when they went to catch the last bus on Sunday night, there was a queue a mile long, so they were left behind and had to stay Sunday night too. Evelyn rang up to the Butcher's at the end of our street to ask him to let my mother know they were staying, and then we all went to bed and they had to catch the 6.15 train to Huddersfield via Leeds. They were up at 5.00 and caught the train quite easily but when they changed at Leeds the train was in, but the porter would not let them go through without a ticket. So while they were booking, the train was due out, and when Hilda got on platform eight the train set off, so she had the guard stopping the train, and when she looked round Evelyn was on another platform so she shouted out to her, and the guard was playing hell but they did not bother as long as they got on the train, they had both to go straight to work then. Hilda has gone again to Ilkley yesterday, but she is staying for three weeks this time.

Well enough of Ilkley, now we'll get down to business. I had a hectic night, last night. I went with my friend and her husband. Of course we went drinking, and a friend of Jim's came over to us, he was in the R.A.F. and he stayed with us all the time up to going home. Then he insisted on taking me home, so I let him. I marched him in the house and my mother nearly dropped, however he stayed talking to my father until 1.30 this morning and then he rang up for his pal to fetch him home. He is coming up for me tonight in the car and he has asked our Evelyn to go with us also, so I think he seems pretty fair, don't you? I will write and let you know how we go on. He goes back to Filey at 2.30 early in the morning but he has 14 days leave on Aug 12, so if I am still with him and I get on nights I will bring him to Sheffield. Of course, don't let the gang into it.

I presume Fanny will be in Scotland having it by now. I hope she does not get into a tight corner this week because Hopkinsons will go mad if she happens anything. I guess there will be a row now if Nellie asks for her release. Emily and I had a real time getting our holiday money. Nobody knew anything about it, and Marflit told us it was going through, the dirty double crosser. We had to go in the Office and see the chief and he said we were not entitled to any, but we told him Mr Wright had promised it to us. Eventually we got £2.15.0 but no thanks to Marflit. In future we are going to the right place when we want to know anything, and to hell with Marflit and the foremen. We were in the main Office forty minutes fighting for our money and nobody knew anything about us at all.

I think I will draw to a close now. Did I tell you my Sweetheart said you was a hedge gutter sniper when I told him about you. I am sorry I cannot make a Rhyme up to put on your envelope but maybe I will for your next letter. I hope so. You will be very quiet these days and busy also by the sound of things. I wish I was back Welding with you, but when I come I shall want to have a try, because by the time the plant is ready I shall have forgotten what bit I knew about Welding.

I will say Cheerio and All the Best.
'Had a good week end?' 'I hope!'
Yours Very Sincerely
Aimeeeeeeeee x

25 'I wish Hitler was in bleeding Hell'

15 Chestnut Street,
Sheepridge

Thursday [late July 1942]

Dear Miss Pearson,

Hello my little hedge gutter sniper, 'what has gone wrong with the mail this week?' I have rushed home every night expecting a letter from you, but it has been in vain.

I went with my Harry, the Air Force boy on Sunday in the car and my sister went with his friend just to make the party up. We called and had a couple of drinks together and then I had a cuddly Woodly, very nice. I received a letter from him yesterday so I have put it in to see what you think about it.[63] He is a very nice boy, I mean man, because he is 37 years old but he does not look it, honest. He has some lovely dark curly hair. In fact I am seriously thinking of settling down with him if he gives me chance, and I feel sure he will. He will be home on leave for 14 days a fortnight on Tuesday and I shall be on nights during his second week, is not that too bad. I think I shall have to let him come up to bed me during the day, 'what do you think?'

Well my dear, I think we are going on piecework next week, because we have had the rate-fixer up, timing us this afternoon.[64] I suppose your dad will have told you what a cushy job they all have, except the volunteers and they are working like hell in readiness for the Welding Plant (if ever?). I am in a very poor way today Miss Pearson, I am sorry to say. I have had a hectic week what with the Ripplay[65] one night and Sirens the next, I have had to get up 3 nights on ARP duty from 2.00 a.m. until about 3.30 each time so I am buggered up now.[66] I wish Hitler was in bleeding Hell. It is now 6.20 and I am going up to the Pictures for seven, so you will have to excuse a short letter this time, love.

[63] It is interesting that Valentine also becomes privy to other correspondences. See above for the copy of the letter Agnes sent to her mother, forwarded to Valentine. Agnes also showed her letters from Jack to Valentine, and there are several references of the women at both Hopkinsons and Brown showing letters from Valentine to each other.

[64] See p. 20 for discussion of their initiatives to get a rate for their work that would allow bonus pay.

[65] I have not been able to trace this reference.

[66] Air Raid Precaution duty.

I am saving up now for our glorious night to be spent together in Huddersfield, so please don't forget that date. I was disappointed when you did not come to Hopkinsons with your dad. Enid said you was coming too, and I had fair built up on seeing you, in fact I had a few Paynes Poppets for you out of my rations, but I have since eaten them.[67] I will close now as I must get to the Pictures for seven, because I have to be in bed for ten on account of that bleeder Hitler, you know you cannot burn the candle at both ends. Please return Harry's letter in your next one to me, will you.

Cheerio Goodnight and Godbless,
Yours Very Sincerely
Aimeeeee

[67] Payne's Poppets are a kind of sweet.

26 Keeping each man in his rabbit hutch

15 Chestnut St,
Sheepridge

Friday [July/August]

My Dear Vagrant,

Just a line thanking you for your most welcome letter, of course you have not put your address on it, so I presume you will get this one when you are ready for returning to Sheffield.[68]

First of all I will report all the happenings at Hopkinsons. We have all ended up in the Staff Canteen again for Lunch, and believe me Lady Marflit is very cross over it, because it is the man in charge over the Canteen who has given us permission, so she cannot throw us out again, until they have enlarged the other one.[69] I had to see Marflit over my Income Tax this morning. They took me 7/7 off last week and the same again this, so I have played hell because I have only £2.17.8. to pay this time, I showed it to you, if you remember. Anyhow I think they must have got across with Enid and me at the Tax Office, and they have slammed £8.15.0 by my name so I have to have an hour off tomorrow to see about it. Believe me, I am unlucky.

Fanny has been at home poorly all the week. Enid says she has some lumps at the back of her neck or something, so I shall try and see her on Sunday. Yes I think it is true about the little offspring so what will Hops have to say about it I wonder. Emily is poorly also and she did not turn up today. I turned up 3/4 of an hour late this morning, owing to being up on Ripplay and Sirens during the night. I expect you will have heard they were at Leeds and have they given them a pasting. Dad has just told me there were 86 killed on a night shift at Forge works, Kirkstall, also Armley Station and Bramley Tram Sheds. So they got some hammer don't you think. Nellie is beginning on Monday. She saw Marflit last week, and she told her to have another week, because they had nothing for her to do, what do you think about that? We have heard that the men are playing hell over the women welders, so it looks like more trouble for us.

---

[68] Valentine had probably written from one of her trips away to see Gottfried.
[69] Because there wasn't enough room for the women in the shop floor canteen, they had been given permission to sit in the Managers' Staff Canteen, which displeased Mrs Marflit.

Alec is home for another seven days embarkation, can you beat that? The girls, I mean sisters, had a real time at Blackpool and they have had nearly all their hair cut off, I had a good laugh when I saw them. I went to meet Chick as I told you last Saturday afternoon, and when I got home at tea-time Harry was on 48 hours leave and he had had tea with mother. What a shock I had! Anyhow everything went OK. I have only two on just now, so I keep them both in their own rabbit hutch. Glad you like the photos but he is sweeter now, because they are rather old ones of him. I have no recent ones of him. I got my hair Permanent Waved last Monday so I am in the front row glamour girls once again. Sorry you have landed in a poor place, but never mind when you come in here we will make up for lost time, all being well. Tell your dad that I must be doing my work well, because Mr Wright came to see me yesterday and he wants me to stay where I am. Also Arthur, my Foreman, says I can stay on days for good if I would stop. But I have not decided yet, but nights don't go down too well for me. They are going to have three shifts in the Welding: 6 until 2, 2 until 10 and 10 until 6, and are the girls carrying on about it. Well I have talked up now so I will get to bed before Gerry comes because I am on Ripplay again tonight.[70] I am going to get your blouse tomorrow but I will wait until you return to Sheffield before I send it to you, because you may cross on the way. Here's wishing you Many Happy Returns of The Day and All The Best. Sorry about the York job, but better luck next time.

Yours Very Sincerely

Amy with Love xxx

P.S. Please Excuse Pencil but I have to hurry and I make blots with ink if I hurry.

Goodnight and Godbless you. Will send some notepaper to Sheffield later. Harold wishes to be remembered to you, he is just on with some Needlework, bless him. By the way we are holding a party on Tuesday night for the Sheffieldites and Harold is the Host. He has told Enid to bring Cyril, so imagine what a time we shall have with those two, and eight of us. I will be thinking about you and wishing you was here too.

---

[70] Gerry was short for German.

27   *Agnes's pregnancy*

15 Chestnut St,
Sheepridge,
Huddersfield

5 September 1942

Dear Vagrant

Hello dear, 'how are you?' Glad to know your time is expired down there, I guess. We had your dad to see us last Tuesday and he had the Caravan with him, my words what a marvellous job you have made of it.[71] I have not seen one to come up to yours. As for ours, well I will not speak about it now after seeing yours. I have sent a release form in today because I am fed up: I have had 7/7 off again for Income Tax and Marflit does not seem to be doing anything about it. I have drawn three pounds this week for working 58 hours and the others have £2.15.0 for 48, so don't you think there ought to be an alteration? I am getting between 900 and 1000 plates out a week. I don't expect to get my release at all, but they will have to get my Income Tax settled up for me before I settle down. Jenny has put in for her release again, but has heard nothing yet. I am looking forward to seeing you in Huddersfield. Now I don't think the Welding Plant will be long but I think you will realise I was right when I said another month. I guess it will be a fortnight yet. We had a very enjoyable evening last Tuesday. I thought about you and wished you was with us, but maybe I will fix another so that you can be present. I think they all had a good time and all at home enjoyed themselves. Fanny was not present but I sent her word. She is still on the sick. I am going to try and see her on Sunday, if at all possible. Excuse pencil but I am in a hurry as usual, I am going to meet Chick tonight. Lovely, I have not seen him all week but I got a letter from him yesterday. An hour from now and I shall be (having it) (a cuddley Woodley). Ah, ah, you thought I meant a bit of Agnes's stuff didn't you? No, I could not do to be like her or else there would be trouble at this establishment. I hope you received your Birthday card in time because I sent it off last Sat. Harold and Mother have gone to the Theatre tonight. I am going to knock off writing now to get ready for my lover. Please find enclosed some notepaper, also the blouse I promised you, and I hope it will be presentable, but it is the best I could do for you, and so please accept the same with My Best Wishes,

Yours Very Sincerely

Amy with Love xx

---

[71] Valentine had painted her parents' caravan in a romantic forest 'camouflage' design.

28   *More tax worries*

15 Chestnut Street,
Sheepridge,
Huddersfield

Sunday [early September 1942]

Dear Miss Pearson,

As I am having such a lot of trouble with my Income Tax.
I wonder if you could let me know my earnings at Sheffield from
Feb 2nd. My first wage paid to me was the 5th of February until
April 5th. It says on my Tax paper I have earned [£]58 from
October until April 5th and I have £2.17s.8d to pay, £9.10.0 @
6/6 in the pound. But they have sent word to Hopkinsons to deduct
off my wage to the amount of £8.15.0. Believe me, I am nearly
going wrong in my head with the damned thing. Enid had £8.15.0
to pay you know, and I think they have made a mistake and slammed
it onto my name. I just finished paying for one £4.17.11, the day
I left Welding rods and I was the only one paying then, but Enid
has got a new one for about [£]3 while she was working at Sheffield
but the £8.15.0 has not turned up yet. Emily has got the last one
and the new one £4.15.0 and [£]3 also Alice has got the new one
[£]3 but not the old one £7.10.0. I hate to put you about but I
want to get it straightened out. I saw Mr Wright on Saturday
morning and he was on about my release and he wanted to know
what my trouble was. So I told him I was doing my best for them,
but they could not do me a good deed and I mentioned about Marflit
always going to see to things for us, and that she was seeing to my
Income Tax and she had not done a thing and that it had been going
on for three weeks now. He has told me I have to take my Income
Tax Forms in to him in the morning and he will attend to them. I
am going on piece-work. I have to see him, so my release is now
withdrawn although I knew I would not get my release. He was
very nice to me though and no sarcasm like Jenny.

Yes, Miss Pearson, it is true poor Fanny is expecting. She
has been to the Doctors and it seems those lumps on her neck will
not go unless she has perfect rest and quietness, but yet she has to
do plenty of walking because of the baby, so I guess she will be in
a fix. What of Hopkinsons? There will be another riot when they
find out. I saw Frank last night and he told me about her so I am
going to see her on Wednesday evening. Nellie is working, I
am pleased to say. She is on a machine with a man and young lady

just watching them, like Fanny was. Our dinnertime sing-song seems to be off nowadays. I expect the old witch will have been playing hell over us to Nellie but we have not said anything to her about it, we go for a walk round these days. We are very well in with the men, now. Emily was cutting one of them his hair on Friday. She made a good job of it too. Well Miss Pearson [when] you come to Huddersfield, we shall have to visit Fanny it seems, because she is on the club. I bet Jack will be upset about her. If she does not alter he will find her in bed when he comes home next month. You will have to send her a catalogue now for Expectant mothers. I think you had better send me one too because I am 4 days late but I think there is a chance yet because I ache back and front. I wish I was coming to Sheffield tomorrow. Anyhow if you don't come to Hopkinsons before next month, Emily and I are going to take a day off and visit you. What will your father say about that? I guess he will keep it dark.

Well Miss Pearson, I will close now and look forward to a nice long letter in return. Let me know if you have received my parcel. I have a date on at 7.00 p.m. and it is now 5.50 and I am neither washed nor dressed and it is Sunday but I have not been near the door. Ma is just nagging at me to get washed so I will close and get ready for a drink or two, we are going over to our Frank's so will sure to be on the spree.

Cheerio Love
            All The Best From
                  Aimeeeee

29   *The price of real love*

15 Chestnut Street,
Sheepridge

Friday, 5.45 p.m. [11 Sept 1942]

Dear Vagrant,
    Thank you so much for your most welcome letter. I have
been on a sweat all the week, wondering if the blouse had not arrived,
because I ought to have registered it but I could not, with it being
Sunday when I posted it, and believe me I had a devil of a time getting
the stamps to stick on anyway I am pleased it is OK for you.
Anytime you want any notepaper give me the wire and I will keep
you going. Please do not mention the blouse to the girls because I
have not told them anything about it and strange to say they keep
asking me if I have heard from you but I told them No. You see I
cannot let them read my letters because I have always some names
in of men and I would not like them to know about Chick or else
they would have a fit. So you will understand why I don't want them
to know all and besides they are jealous of Fanny and you, and they
know I am thick with Fanny and that's enough for them.
    Well dear, about the Welding you will be surprised to hear
we have all put a rod in for Mr Robinson.[72] He said mine was a
good one and that you could always tell by the slag on top. As for
the others I was not there when they put one in. There is one machine
ready, but that is all. But the others will not be long, Mr Robinson
says, so maybe I will be seeing you before very long. I hope so anyway.
    Please may I convince you that it is quite correct about
Fanny. I shall be seeing her this weekend, all being well. I saw Frank
last week and he told me it was correct, so we had better start knitting.
Glad to inform you that I am quite in order, I think I must have
strained myself with lifting and I have done some this week. I
have been on piecework. The rate fixer came up last Monday and
what a bugger he is. I have been getting 160 plates out per day and
now I have to get 205 plates out per day and I get 8/- per week
extra. It's bleeding horse work, but it's not going to come off next
week. Believe me, I have come home at 7.30 half dead. I have just
washed me and looked at the evening paper and gone straight to
bed, buggered. Plums, we have had pounds of them. We go shopping
every dinnertime just the same as at Sheffield. We have holiday a

---

[72] Mr Robinson was their very popular supervisor.

week on Monday Sept 21st, so if you are at work, I will pop over and see you again, if its OK. If not, just let me know will you please, but make it in your way to be at Welding Rods for once. I should have had tomorrow afternoon off this week, but they have put it to next Saturday so that it will seem a long holiday, the devils.

I had a meeting with Chick again, but I have had to cancel it. I am mad. We spent a marvellous evening together last Friday. Honestly speaking, lots of love was not in the running, he was lovely. I bet he will be mad when he gets my letter putting him off for tomorrow. He is still very much in love. It is his Birthday a week on Wed, but I don't know what he wants. There is one thing he does want more than anything (real love), ha ha. I am going to give in though before long, if things don't alter at Hopkinsons. I am just in the mood. Maybe it is as well I am not seeing him tomorrow because I should not hesitate to let him (have it). I don't give a bugger what happens nowadays. I absolutely loath Hopkinsons anyway, as far as gas cutting is concerned. I am definitely not stopping on that machine. I AM GOING WELDING. They have upset the applecart this week.

I hope you have enjoyed your holiday, have you? I hope you have not been on the wet grass, but it sounds as though you have if you have got a cold, so please don't blame your mother. Nellie is getting out of Welding if she can I think, because she does not feel well enough, anyhow I am more than willing to step into it. I have not had any more words with Marflit lately, but I am expecting words with somebody if there is not more wage in my packet next week. I will have done all the plates they needed by next Thurs, so I will [be] all set for Welding and I will go on that machine that is ready if they will let me. Honest I am having a fit for fear they put me on some other jobs to cut out. Tell your father to demand my presence in the Welding, will you please?[73]

What is your idea of red and blue ink? I must say you are very patriotic, (I wonder). Or was it the pen that knocked, or maybe the blue ink wanted filling up? I think I will wash me and go out for a short while now and get a tonic. I am not feeling too well yet, believe me I have been half dead this last fortnight. I have lost a lot of weight lately and yesterday I had my ulcer pains again. Was it the plums or the pears, or was it love? What do you think (ha ha)? Well love, I will have to close now, so cheerio and all the very best to you and yours.

---

[73] This is one of the striking passages in the letters, for its uncompromising expression of the desire to get on with welding.

P.S. Let me know if I shall be welcome a week on Monday or if you prefer to go hedgebottoming. I have to take Mother to Ilkley next Sat and carry the luggage. I shall stay until Sunday, but if you are away again I shall spend Monday there too, so let me know please as soon as you can.

> Lots of Love from
> Aimeeeee

Note paper seems to be going with a swing here tonight. I had no idea I had written you so much but maybe you will write a bit more next time. I hope so, because I soon read through tonight's. My mother wants to know if I am here for the night. I guess I could go on all night, if I told you all that went off at work. Anyway I don't like to bore you so I will ring off. Harold has gone to Ilkley until Sunday, so I will give him your love when he comes home. He seems to be like me looking for letters from you, he was asking me why you had not written on Tuesday. He said had you crossed me off? I told him he knew as much about you as I did. Cheerio Love. Excuse Pencil in a hurry.

30 *The night shift*

The New Firm (washout)

[21 Sept 1942]
Monday 9.30 p.m.

Dear Vagrant,
Just a line to let you know I arrived home safely at 7.15 p.m.
Mother had not much to say fortunately. I told her all the Hairdressers
were closed so I made my mind up to go to Sheffield, and then I
gave her my sweets and everything was OK. I got washed and changed
straight away, then I put my dinner up and took my dog out, and
by the time I had performed these duties it was time to report here.
I am sorry to say I forgot about my tea so you will have an idea how
I feel, what with an empty stomach and tired a little, and most of
all from my wrist to my elbow is all burnt with Welding and it is
burning like bleeding hell and as red as a beetroot, where I had hold
of the shield in my left hand. I have just asked Eddie what time we
have some lunch and he said we only stop at two until 2.30 a.m. so
I said 'the hell I am having some bleeding lunch right now'. So I
have put the pan on, we have a small secret gas ring in our department
you see, so I am going to make good use of it.
I must thank you for a very enjoyable day Miss Pearson,
it's been lovely and I shall come again before long. Don't worry,
honest I will be thinking about you all night tucked in bed fast asleep
and poor little me working like bleeding hell. If my letter seems all
jumbled up you must excuse me because I have to keep breaking
off, and doing a bit of work, to keep the production up, you know
there's a war on.
Eddie is just oiling the machine for me. I have just had a
pint of coffee and a sandwich and once again I feel as fit as a fiddle
and ready for anything. There is quite a splash in the paper about
our Harold.[74] I will forward it on for you to look at, at a later date.
I have cut 21 plates up to now and it's only eleven so I will have to
go steady or else I am going to do more than I do in the daytime.
I have got Fanny's letter here with me so she will get it as soon as
she arrives in the morning. All the girls in the next department are
singing away like nightingales. Oh to be back at Welding Rods!

---

[74] This may have been connected to Harold, Amy's brother's, work as a teacher
in business studies, or his unusual skills as an embroiderer and cook.

I wish I had never seen this bleeding place. I'll admit it was a bit boring at times over there, but believe me, it is just as bad here. I hope you are feeling OK after your Pommies.[75] I wish I had a few here just now, could I knock them back. What with the damned Blackouts and the hot sparks I am sweating like a bull (no not John Bull). Ha ha, the old rat never spoke to me today, and I am so worried (what do you think?). Honest it did feel grand to set foot in the good old firm this morning, I felt quite at home and really you was very attentive towards me and am I looking forward to your stay in Huddersfield it cannot come too soon, and I am looking forward to showing you round also. I guess Fanny will be very annoyed tomorrow when she hears of my trip to Sheffield, especially if she has had nothing to do. The girls will have quite a shock when I convey your love and best wishes to them. I am just dying for 7.30 a.m. when I will give them a rude awakening. Their eyes will pop out, saying nothing about mine at the moment. If your father rung up to Hops maybe they gave him some idea when the plant will be ready. If so, just let us know what they say, will you, and then I will keep a good look out and see how they are framing. Well, I have nothing more to say as I talked up at Sheffield and I will have to go next door with my pot ready for my tea at 12.00 o'clock. Once again thanks for everything, and the envelope is one found at home, so don't think I have left Hops (what a chance I have). My Eyes are dim I cannot see I've only got one pair of specks with me.[76] Goodnight Love and Godbless. Sweet Dreams.

> With Love from
> Amy xxx

P.S. Don't forget to keep it dark to the girls about my secret Lover (for the love of Mike), another saying like cut your water off.

---

[75] Probably a kind of cider.
[76] The lines are from a popular wartime song.

31 The mysterious disappearance of Agnes[77]

15 Chestnut Street,
Sheepridge,
Hudd

Saturday 1.30 p.m., [early October 1942]

My Dear Vagrant,

I have had a very exciting morning and I thought I had better inform you right away. Mrs Marflit came up to me and said, somebody wished to see Amy from Sheffield and presumed it was me. I went down and who should be there, but Agnes's sister Pat. She wanted to know if I had seen Agnes last night, I said no I had not been out all week. It seems she was out with a girl named Elsie and she left her at 9.50 to catch a bus for her mother's and nothing has been heard of Agnes since. Pat said that she was heartbroken, because Jack's leave was cancelled again, but strange to say Jack came home last night but he has to go back tomorrow evening. Believe me, I am very upset. But don't you worry yet, because I am going up tomorrow afternoon to see if she has turned up. I cannot go today because I have promised to go with Evelyn to Alec's mother's to tea. I will give you a ring at 12.35 on Monday if there should be any bad news, but I hope to goodness there is not. Honest Miss Pearson, I shall never rest until I know she is safe. I told the girls and Emily said 'oh she will be at Sheffield'. I don't mind where she is, but I do hope she is safe and well.

Well my dear, work [h]as gone down very well and we have made 10/- on top of £2.15.0, so we are satisfied, because we know we shall earn more next week. Mr Robinson has got us 1¾ hrs per bracket plus 15 per cent Bonus. I have done some good ones this week, and if I get a bit more confidence in myself I shall do better, Mr Robinson says. Alec is coming home for 48 hrs next week end. By the way how did you like the Rhyme. I sent it to Evelyn. I fetched my costume back from being cleaned last night and my friend has made a real good job of it. I am thinking of putting it on this afternoon. I guess at this moment you will be enjoying a cuddley woodly with G. I have not seen Chick, nor heard from him since the Tuesday you was at Hops. I cannot tell what has happened. What with the worry over him and then Fanny, I am just about in a trance, so you must please excuse all mistakes and writing because I am writing

---

[77] See Letter 15 for Agnes's version of this escapade.

(26)

15 Chestnut Street
Sheepridge
Hudd. Sat 1.30m

My Dear Vagrant,

I have had a very exciting morning and
I thought I had better inform you right away. Mrs
Marfelt came up to me and said, somebody wished
to see Amy from Sheffield and presumed it was me.
I went straight down and who should be there but
Agnes's sister Pat. She wanted to know if I had
seen Agnes last night, I said no I had not been
out all week. It seems she was out with a girl
named Elsie and she left her at 9-50 to catch a
bus for her mother's and nothing has been heard
of Agnes since. Pat said that she was heartbroken
because Jack's leave was cancelled again, but
strange to say Jack came home last night but
he has to go back tomorrow evening believe me
I am very upset but dont you worry yet because
I am going up tomorrow afternoon to see if she
has turned up. I cannot go today because I
have promised to go with Evelyn to Alec's mother's
to tea. I will give you a ring at 12-35 on Monday
if there should be any bad news, but I hope
to goodness there is not, honest Miss Pearson
I shall never rest until I know she is safe. I

this any style. I am looking forward to seeing you again before long, because I might not live very long now I am fixed to a welding plant all day long. I have already developed a shocking cold but hope it does not last long, because I cannot have any Rum to cure it. I have turned good all at once, I am teetotal and don't swear, from now on, and I now say my prayers every night. That is owing to my Welding, I really am taking the job serious and I am going to stick at it until I am as good as you, and then is the time to fly my kite and have a good time. Until then I am a good girl, unless I see you in the meantime and then maybe I would soften for a few drinks. Harold has taken my mother to Bradford for the day and I shall have to close now because I have that Brown Boiler Suit to patch before I go out today ready for Monday. I hope you are in the best of health, also your mother and father. I will write you again on Monday and let you know about Fanny. Kind Regards to you from the Family.

> Yours Very Sincerely,
> Amy xx
> With Love

PTO Sunday 2.20

Hello here I am again. I am just about to go up to Fanny's. I have just laid all my things ready for work in the morning as I have to meet Frank at 7.00, for the last time I hope. I have also to meet Nancy, the girl who was with us the other Monday, and am trusting Fanny and Jack will go with us, that is if she has returned. What a to-do! Harry has just arrived and I am as black as fireback. I will have to take him up to Fanny's, so what is going to happen now I don't know. Frank and Nancy will both be at the same place waiting for me, and poor Harry here. I am in a real jam now. I wish you was here to help me out. I don't want Frank now and I must go meet Nancy because we had arranged to go over to our Frank's and he will go mad if I don't meet her, so I will let you know how things turn out. I must ring off now and get changed.

Cheerio Love and think about me tomorrow when I have got over tonight. I will put round the envelope if Fanny has turned up. So long x

32   *Valentine 'Vagrant'*

15 Chestnut Street,
Sheepridge,
Huddersfield

[mid–October 1942]

My dear Vagrant,
          Hello you dirty stay-out all night. Under Hedgebottoms, in tents, and now in Lavatories, where will it be next? Jail I should imagine. Ha Ha, to think I was under the impression you was spending a week away again, when I did not hear from you all last week. Anyway my letter spent a dirty night out instead of coming to Sheepridge. Only this afternoon I told Mr Robinson you must be away again as I had not heard from you for over a week. But I am pleased to hear you are still in Sheffield.
          Enid the nasty cat, telling you about my swearing![78] Well let me inform you she is doing a big share herself these days. I have given up nearly since that afternoon because Mr Robinson was disgusted. Also he does not like girls who drink, so for his benefit I have given up all these bad habits, and believe me it has not taken much doing. Honest, I would give up anything for him because he is a real good boss. I could fall for him, believe me. Emily and me love him but he does not know. The girls do though, in fact I am surprised Enid has not told you in her letter because Emily and me plague her life out over your father. I am up in the far cubicle this week at the top of Tank Alley on my own and I am fed up. It's like been in jail but only another three days to go and then it's Enid's turn. I have much pleasure in telling you my eye is better thank you. I have had a new experience today, some slag went in my ear, I nearly went mad, I could not get it out. Mr Robinson calls me
The Mighty Atom.
          Next time you write, will you put that on the envelope? It will cause a real scream amongst the others, especially Chris because it tickles him to death. Emily and I had our Photos taken again yesterday and really they are good ones, better than the last. Chris is framing one tonight to hang up at work. Under Emily, he is going to put 'Wildcat' and under me 'Mighty Atom'.
          I went to the Canteen Staff Dance on Saturday night. I had a real time and what do you think? I won the Spot Waltz Prize: a pair of Mauve Satin French Knickers and my partner won 60 Capstan Cigarettes. Just imagine the look on my face, when I opened my parcel

[78] See Enid's Letter 53.

to show him what I had won. I went crimson and I did not know where to put myself. Ah ah, I bet you wish you had seen me. Sydney Wright was there but he did not stay late. I had a partner all night, I did enjoy myself. If Chick knew he would go mad. He thinks I have given up but he will not get to know. I had a lovely evening last Friday with him, he was making violent love in the shop doorway next to the Picturedrome until the bus came. Honestly he is getting worse and he fears nobody. Two or three fellows spoke to him in the bus and he sits by me as cheeky as brass and always helps me off. I get more ashamed each time I see him, but nothing on earth will make me give up with him, I love him more than ever. I am meeting him again on Thursday, same place.

Thank you very much for the Arc Eye prescription. I will get some at my earliest convenience. We are all on time wage this week welding the <u>bars in</u>. I have not seen Fanny for a fortnight. I bet she is cursing me but I have been otherwise engaged, and also being I have given up drinking it's no good looking her up. I have not tasted any drink for three whole weeks. Don't you think I have done well? Well my dear how are you getting on? I presume you are well because you don't mention anything different in your letter. Nellie is turning into a dirty girl. She brought a dirty paper to us today. I will copy it from her when I can find time. By the way love, I have found that dirty Rhyme in my drawer about the alphabet 'A for the artful word he uses', and so on. Do you want it? If so, let me know in your next letter and please don't be as long in writing next time because I wonder all sorts of things.

I think I have talked up now, love. Father and Mother are on the Settee warming their pretty toes, Evelyn is cutting a dress out in the kitchen, Hilda is at Harry's, and Harold at Tech. Your Highness is now about to wash her and have supper, then to bed. We were all in bed for 10.00 p.m. last night and we slept over until 7.5 this morning but I just checked 7.33 and they allowed two minutes so I will have 15 minutes off for one but why worry, I had a good rest.[79] Well I will close now love, wishing you all the best.

Goodnight and Godbless You
Yours Sincerely,
Amy x

P.S. Please let me know if your paper has run out because I will send you some more. I have had to borrow some tonight. Too tired to go upstairs for some.

---

[79] Presumably, she had to work 15 minutes for the one minute counted out of her three minutes late for work.

33   *Welding at last*

Dear Miss Pearson,
          Mr Robinson has told me today that you are coming over
next Tuesday for a week and believe me I could have squeezed him,
I was that thrilled. I have written and told Mrs Helme. Sorry about
the mistake but aircraft is overhead, and I am just wondering if we
are going to have the Sirens. I guess we shall be having our night
out either Wed or Thurs. We had better let you get moved in first.
I have arranged with a friend of mine to put us up, so I think
everything will be in order. You can come up to our depot for tea
and then we can pick the two Franks up, also Fanny. That is if it is
alright to you but you will let me know. Fanny insists we don't go
home, so it looks as though we are in for a real good time. The reason
I have made arrangements for us to sleep out up this quarter is because
if our Frank takes us to Clifton we shall be four miles nearer here
than Moldgreen where Agnes lives so we don't want to be walking
all night (do we?). Ha Ha, I hope to have you blind you (skunk?)
I mean to do my stuff this time. I have been waiting for this chance
for some time but we shall get batting before 8.50 this time, so watch
yourself. Our Frank [may] be trying to cobble you if he gets fresh.
I am going to send word for him to reserve next Wed or Thursday
and he will be fixed. He has been looking forward to meeting you
because I have told him all about you. Whatever we do, we must
not let the girls know or else Fanny and I shall be in the soup again.
          I am Welding at last but Alice and Enid have not arrived
yet. Mr Robinson is very good to us and I am sure we shall make
a go of it for him. I am trying my very best to please him and I made
a good start this morning. But I regret to say that I made a few slagholes at tea-time, but he said it did not matter, he would attend to
them, bless him. I have never met a better foreman in my life than
Mr Robinson. He is a real gentleman and I will not let him down
at any cost. I only wish he would swear at me a bit for making a
mess of a few odd runs but he says it's just with being out of practice.
I will do some real beauties tomorrow or else I will eat my shirt.
Don't worry, I shall not let Welding Rods down. This is all I have
to say for the present so Cheerio, here is to next week.
          Yours Very Sincerely
               Aimeee

PS Excuse Pencil in a hurry again. The Sirens have not gone yet so
I presume they are our Aircraft Goodnight and Godbless.

34 Slag burns and family news

15 Chestnut Street,
Sheepridge

Tuesday, [October/November 1942]

Dear Vagrant,

Many thanks for you[r] letter which gave me quite a shock coming so soon, but believe me it was welcome. I was afraid it contained bad news, but I am glad to know you have got over the weekend safely. I was a trifle worried over you, when I left you in the train. I wish I had gone as far as Brighouse with you now, because Frank made me go for a drink with him and it was 9.30 when I got home but thank goodness I had washed up and cleared away when the others came in. Father was in but he never said a word. I wish I had seen you laid on the mat. I sure would have tormented you, but maybe one of these days when Chick and I are having a weekend off, we shall bump into you. I hope so.

You ask me about the Welding. I am pleased to inform you that I have made good progress this week, and Mr Robinson is very pleased. He says I want to have more confidence, anyhow I am pleased with myself because I really was worried last week. By the way, I gave him your message and he said, he was sorry but he had no idea you was leaving on Friday, and his son called for him at 5.00 o'clock so he went straight home with him (hard luck).

We really are in the money. We did eleven brackets up to 5.00 o'clock tonight so as we cannot do any brackets extra. We shall just get the 15 per cent Bonus which will amount to 8/- on top of £2.14.3. Hopkinsons want blowing up, the skinny blighters.

We have all been knocked up with the heat today so there is going to be another row before long. I will let you have details in my next letter. Emily has burnt her face with slag so the nurse has plastered it up. Also your pal Aimee is suffering once again with half my face red and the other half white with the damned masks.

Fanny was not well when I went up on Saturday afternoon but she said she went to the Station. I had Enid with me and she went and let the cat out to her about Wed. Oh I was mad, after all we had done to keep it dark, she reeled all off so you can imagine what I felt like. I don't think Enid has said anything to the girls. Anyway they have said nothing to me. My mother was sorry she did not see you but you must come again anytime she says. I am sorry to say she has got a terrible cold. She is just leaned back in the chair having forty winks. Evelyn is knitting away at a jumper, father is darning a small hole in his sock, Hilda has gone to the butcher's, and Harold is at the Technical College. As for Amy, well I have some liver to cook for supper when Hilda comes back and I am to wash yet, believe me I am buggered.

I think Frank and I have finished. But we are on friendly terms you know, I could not be any other [way] after I have spent his sweet rations. Sorry G got a ducking on Saturday I wish I had seen him too I would have laughed I bet he looked good. I say, what about that Photograph are you going to soften or not, I have a frame for it waiting patiently. Please excuse this, my father is sat on the settee with me and he is acting the fool, not for long though because he knows I am in a bad mood. I hope you enjoyed your lunch [at] the Canal side, I wish I had been with you. Don't forget when you have a weekend away from G, come and spend it here. Mother will be pleased to see you anytime, so please remember. I will close now and when I see Chick I will give him your love. I do wish you could have seen him.

Goodnight and Godbless
Yours Very Sincerely With Love,
Aimeeee xx
All The Best

I was that peeved with my hair yesterday, I had father cutting it last night. SHORT BOB. My curl at the front [h]as all broken off. It's only two inches long and it just hangs over my face like a donkey fringe. No longer peroxide, no more.

9.45. Please find enclosed a ditty handed to me from the forces. While I am writing this Harold wants to know what you have to say. I said 'wait a minute'! He says, 'what did she say that for'! He has just come in, so I will give him a few extracts from your letter and then to bed. I have got washed and had my Supper. Goodbyeeeee

35   *A sit-down strike*

15, Chestnut Street,
. Sheepridge,
Huddersfield

Sunday 12.30 a.m. [November 1942]

Dear Vagrant,

Thank you very much for all your nice letters to hand yesterday, I guess you had a real time making them all follow on. I did not expect you sending them all on right away, but I do thank you very much for doing so, all the same. I have had a very nice quiet weekend. Emily, Alice and her friend and I went to the Ritz Cafe for tea yesterday, to see our old pal Jenny. We fair enjoyed ourselves. We left there and went to the Market, and who should we bump into, but Mr Wright and his wife and child. He was pushing the pram up King Street. He raised his hat and said good afternoon to us, what do you think about that? Yes definitely Frank is off, he was waiting at the wrong place last Sunday so when he asked me to go with him this weekend, I just said 'oh no you are not making a fool of me again' and left him at that. I went to a show with the company I was with yesterday. I should have met Harry at 7.00 but I have crossed him off too. So once again I am almost free to do as I please. I have to go to Emily's to tea today, also Jenny, so I am hurrying to get off for 2.00 o'clock before Harry shows up again.

I am being true to Chick now for a short while because if he keeps hearing tales about the Welders of Hopkinsons he will always be getting hurt. I met him yesterday afternoon for an hour before I met Emily. Yes he has come round, trust me to bring him too. He heard the men saying we had a sit down strike, and that the girl with glasses on, pink ones, said 'bugger it I am going home'. So he was upset to think I had been swearing. Anyhow I told him it was a lie and he said he was glad it was, because he did not want me to start cursing like men, goodness knows it was bad enough for him, me working amongst them, without talking like them. However all is well now and I meet him again next Friday. Honest if he knew how much I did swear he would go mad, but I will watch he does not hear anymore about me. I will see if I cannot control my feelings a bit in future.

Yes my dear, we have got a new bib and brace overall each, except Alice. We have such a performance when we go to the corner, having to take the boiler suit off, we thought we would have a change. So we all step in, in new Battle dress tomorrow. Mr Robinson is still his same sweet self. Emily and I have fallen in love with him in fact we make mistakes so we can fetch him off each other. He wants to meet Fanny very much. He has heard such a lot about her, but Emily says she will have to go to the top end because she is not going to upset the original five again. In fact, they all hope she does not come back Welding, so when you write about Fanny please put it on a paper to itself because they cannot stick her. Emily told Mr Robinson that she could only talk about one thing all the time and she got on her nerves, Mr Robinson said 'oh I don't like that sort of talk, a lot of the men in the Foundry talked to the girls that way', and that he did not approve of it. So Fanny will have to be like me and reform. Of course I will warn her, so please do not mention to Fanny that they have told Stanley[80] about her or else she will have a fit. I told him she was a blonde bombshell when he asked me about her. I said 'oh you will not be coming to look at me when Fanny comes, she is a real glamour girl'. He said, 'it's Welding I am worried about, can she Weld?' I said 'Definitely she can, as good as anybody here and better than some', he said 'oh that's OK'.

Chris can keep us going very well, we have not had to wait yet. We have turned 30 perfect Brackets out each this week. Can you beat that? I think we'll have about £3.10.0 this week, all being well. Please tell your father that Aimeeee can do them in 3/4 of an hour now and he must not call me a liar because I have three witnesses. Well I will have to cut off now. I am on A.R.P. compulsory training tomorrow night, also next Sunday morning. I have also been on Ripplay all weekend once again, but it has not gone off for two nights. I hope it does not go off tonight, ou[r] last night on duty. Thank the Lord I am exempt from Firewatching.

How is the Bull getting along? I hope he is still his sweet self. I am afraid I shall not be able to knock a day and come and see you now because they send forms round to see why you are late or why you have had a day off. I nearly knocked last Thursday. I was very dizzy when I got out of Bed but I pulled myself together and managed to go to work. Mr Robinson told me to keep going if possible, so I did. I am much better now all that remains is a very bad cough just like Croup. Well I am going to the Canteen Dance at Hops next Saturday, got two partners already.

Cheerio Love and All The Best
Yours Very Sincerely,
Aimeeee xxx

PS Had a good weekend Have you had it?

---

[80] Mr Robinson.

36   *Going teetotal*

15 Chestnut Street,
Sheepridge,
Huddersfield

Thursday 10.30 p.m. [November 1942]

Dear Vagrant,

Sorry I have not had a letter from you to answer, so I am going to tell you all I know. First on Tuesday night about seven o'clock I had quite a shock. After I had washed myself, my left eye was rather troublesome so I used some Optrex. No response. Borasic Crystals, no response. Golden eye ointment and still no better. After all this I put a tea-leave poultice on, and tied a bandage round. This eased it a little, but oh what pain I had. I could not bear the light, so we took a globe off. Believe me, I was frantic. I got up Wednesday morning with an eye the size of two, but went to work. Mr Robinson sent me to the Ambulance Room and the Nurse said I had to watch it did not turn septic. I had a fit, she said it was burnt in the corner, not with slag. I must have had my mask on one side. Anyway, we have got the new ones now thank you. I had to go to the Ambulance room five times yesterday to have my eye seen to. Mr Robinson did two brackets for me, and Emily did one. He would not let me go home, although I could not see to Weld. I am glad to say it has improved a good deal now, so in future I will look after myself a bit more.

Fanny has not shown up yet and I have not seen her this last week. I should not be surprised if she does not turn up on Monday. I have a feeling she will somehow. What do you think about me going tee-total and giving up swearing? Mr Robinson does not like girls who swear and drink so I must live a good life now. I do like him, Miss Pearson, in fact I think I could fall for him, but I have not a chance. I fair get some good welds down when he comes to look at me. He says he would not part with his girls now at any price, so he must be suited with us. He sits and has a smoke with us sometimes. Of course Emily and I smoke his Cigs. Honest we could not wish for a better boss and we definitely will <u>not</u> work for another. Emily and I are both in love with him. I think he has an idea we all think a lot about him. Chris keeps us going very well, we have not had to wait a minute yet, so you will know how busy he is. Are you still going to see your lover at weekends? I hope you are, but mind what you are doing, I don't want you locking up.

I have seen Frank twice this week and he gave me a ten PKT of Cigs each time, but no dates with him. I have to see Chick tomorrow, 8.00 p.m. by the Picturedrome. I say he was pleased with your letter. He said 'I bet she is a sport like you, anyhow I hope to have the pleasure of meeting her when she comes here again'. I say, the last buses are nine o clock out of Town next week, is not that a Bugger. I shall be doing plenty walking then I think, what do you say.

We have a lovely fire, believe me I don't fancy going to bed and leaving it. I am going to the Canteen Dance on Saturday for a change and I am going to see Annie, my pal at Brighouse, on Sunday. I say Jenny went to Gloucester this morning so we shall be a while before we see her, I expect. I will close now love but will write again on Sunday. Goodnight and Godbless you. Kind regards to Mam and Dad tell him we are keeping up Welding Rods's name.

      Love from
        Aimeeeeee xxx

37   *New bib and brace overalls*

15 Chestnut Street,
Sheepridge,
Huddersfield

[November 1942]

Dear Miss Pearson,

Just a word to let you know I have not been entertaining
Emily this weekend as our Harold is spending his holiday at home
so he has shopped the job. We thought he would be going to
London but he has changed his mind. Emily has a Septic right
wrist, also a septic finger on her left hand so she has as much as she
can manage. Your father asked me last Thursday if Agnes was
coming back to Hopkinsons. I told him yes so far as I knew. It seems
quite evident you have not enlightened him of all the latest
happenings. Anyhow it is perhaps as well. Harold and I are not on
speaking terms since last Thursday we had a set too, so I cannot put
in any message from him this time. I went with Frank last night down
to the White Lion where Agnes's Frank is pianist. I thought maybe
Fanny would be down because I wanted to know when she would
be coming to work but she was not there. Frank says she faints two
or three times a day so things are not looking too good. I am going
up to see her after tea but I shall not go to the club. I opened out
last night and had four Rum-and Gingers. I feel [. . .] anyhow
today.[81] Fancy, the first for a month. I shall have to report in the
morning because Mr Robinson always asks me where I have been.
He said he could see me being a Sunday school teacher in a bit, I
said 'no, in a convent', he said 'oh no, you would upset them all'.

How was it you did not come with your father last Thursday?
I fair expected seeing you also. Enid has been coaching some girls
and boys for a concert, so all the girls from Tank Alley went to watch
it last Friday and we all had tea at Enid's. We fair had a good time
lass, you ought to have been with us. We are on full bang tomorrow
with the Welding. Mr Wright told Mr R he had to put some night
workers on. Of course you will have an idea what we said. We are
not going on nights, so I don't know what will happen, we may
have to start working over before long. I shall be over to see you
again should I happen to be put on nights.

I presume you will be in G's arms at this moment, I hope
so anyway. I am sorry I did not put the Rhyme in for you last week.

---

[81] A word appears to be missing in the original.

I found it in the chair after I had sealed up your letter, so I am putting it in this. Please find enclosed the Photo as promised, trusting you send me one of you in your next letter. I am sorry but I have not seen Chick this week so have not been able to get any notepaper for you yet, but I will send you some this next weekend. I am going to send you the last school book along with this letter so please make it last will you. I am going up to a Concert on Tuesday lunch time at the mill where I used to work. They are giving a show in aid of the Comforts Fund, so maybe I will get to know a bit more about the Secretary. I hope they have made an example of him. I will write again on Wednesday and let you know all the news. I am sorry I don't seem to have much to say this time. I will have to get washed and dressed now and prepare tea, its 4 o'clock. I hope you are in the pink and enjoying your fire-watching, but don't make a beast of yourself with the money you get.

      Cheerio All The Best
        Love From,
          Aimee

P.S. Note our Photo taken in our new Bib and Brace Overalls. Much easier to take off in case of emergency.

38 *Feeling champion enough to get five brackets off*

15 Chestnut St,
Sheepridge

Sunday 12.25 a.m. [November 1942]

My Dear Val,

I have just come downstairs after a real good night's rest. I am spending a quiet week end indoors. I saw Dr Gamm on Friday after waiting from 1.00 p.m. until 4.30 and I just got back to work at 4.45 in time to report to the nurse and Mr Robinson. Your letter filled in some of my waiting time as my mother brought it with her when she met me at dinner time. The Dr never said anything to me at all as to what is wrong but maybe he will inform my own Dr. I am sorry to say I have to go to the Infirmary again tomorrow at the same time. He gave me a real good Examination I also had to have some drops in, blast them. I could hardly see at all then. With my right eye, I could not read the last four lines of letters. I am not blaming the Welding light at all. Like you, I think it is the strain with Welding continually, because these glasses I am wearing are only a good three months [old] so it should not be them. I am sure it is eyestrain because I was seeing very well at Sheffield. Also I was not Welding continually a whole day, so we will see what tomorrow brings. I have not been told to give the job up so I worked yesterday morning and I am working in the morning.

Mr Robinson is very upset about the job and he does not want me to give the job up if I can help it. He came down on Sat morning first thing, and he was pleased to see me. He said 'I never expected you turning in, really I do appreciate you coming, because if you had rested your eyes until Monday afternoon it may have given the Dr a better chance to see what is wrong, anyway you will be able to turn a bit more work out'. It is rather unfortunate because Enid is away poorly so that only leaves three of them. Then I am away but Mr R has no need to worry, because I will not let him down whatever happens, I have told him so. I had some difficulty again on Saturday with a downhand run so he came in and held my hand once again. I have got going nicely now, I just get in a jam now and again with the downhand but apart from that I do very well. I can now do one comfortable in $^{3}/_{4}$ of an hour so we are in clover. I did seven whole brackets last Monday and I did not start until 8.00 a.m. yesterday and I had done three at 11.00 a.m., so I swept up then and had a rest. Our time is now fixed at $1^{3}/_{4}$ hrs per

bracket plus 15 per cent bonus, OK, don't you think? I have got
another ring off Frank. I told him Hilda was wearing my other, so
he said 'well let her keep it, then'. I saw Chick yesterday afternoon
but did not get any note paper. He is going to get it during this week
and will let me have it (the paper) next Friday. I hope you got that
book I sent you because you did not mention it in your letter.

The Secretary has found the £73.5.5$\frac{1}{2}$ and has made the
money missing in order. The Committee gave him a week to find
it, so I don't know where he has got it from. We have never heard
another word about the baby born in the Lavatory. Nellie has never
said anything about Sydney lately. Of course she is on nights again,
so we don't get the chance to have a few words with her. Emily is
still visiting the Ambulance Room three times a day with her wrist.
Alice our dark horse is about the best of the bunch, I doubt if she
has been to the Ambulance room at all. Her friend has brought her
another orange, also a block of Toffee. Mr Robinson has told her
to take all he offers her, he thinks he has a slate off. I say lass, they
are putting absenteeism cards in the slot now when you are away.
Fanny has one and Enid has one also. They are pink ones and, by
what I gather, you have to give them to your Foreman on your return
to work. I think they are going to make a case with those who stay
away without being poorly so maybe I will get one in next. I gave
Marflit a shock, when I went to the Ambulance room for a Voucher
for the infirmary. I told the Nurse the Doctor thought it was
Welding, and that maybe I would have to give it up, and Marflit
was stood there listening in, but she never said a word.

Have you had a good weekend? I hope you have. Glad to
hear G is having leave again. Alec is home again for a few days so
Evelyn is at her own home. How about coming to have a look at
your trainees, you will be surprised when you see our Welding now.
In fact I think we shall knock you out with the shock. Believe me,
Emily is real good and can she knock the brackets back. I have not
seen Fanny nor heard about her yet, but I have arranged to see her
next week. I think she will have lost touch with her welding because
you know what a mess our first brackets were. No Harold and I are
not on speaking terms yet. I am having to go out this afternoon
because he is in for the day. Mother and Dad are going to Frank's
to tea so I am going with them. I am getting good, don't you think.
My words, your girls are getting rather vulgar don't you think? I
don't know how they dare come out with that nasty word, I bet
he was wild. I don't see any chance to come over now they have
put absentee cards in the slot, but the first chance I do get I will be
right over you can bet your life on that.

My Dancing partner wanted me to go Dancing with him again last night but I refused. I have not seen Frank since last Thursday. I dare not see him much because he [is] always after my blood. I feel real champion now after my weekend rest. I think I may get five brackets off before I go to the Infirmary tomorrow, I feel in the mood just now. They had a lovely concert up at the mill where I used to work. On Tuesday Lunch time I went up. Chick was Entertaining and they had got a lovely Choir together. A little boy sang 'England'. It was lovely, better than any of our E.N.S.A. Concerts.[82] I was $\frac{1}{4}$ of an hour late when I got back to Hop's but I had told Mr R I may be late back, he said it was alright. I told him I wished I was back there and he played hell, he says I have not to go up any more and that I have not to ask him for any more time off to go up there if that's how I feel when I come back. I am falling for Mr R more every day, honest my heart fair flutters when he comes into my Cubicle. Really he is goodness itself towards us and he will go out of his way to please us. I am finding it no trouble at all to go to work these days, I am up out of bed like lightning.

Well I must close now love, trusting you are in the best of Health, also Mother and Dad. By the way, did you tell him about my eyes? If so, what had he to say, please? Will write again on Tuesday and give you the news.

Cheerio All The Best,
Love from,
Aimee

---

[82] The Entertainments National Services Association — ENSA — (sometimes known as Every Night Something Awful) provided live entertainment for the troops.

39 *Amy is advised to give up welding*

Monday 8.15 p.m., 9 November 1942

Hello Val,

Well I have been to the Infirmary this afternoon and they can do nothing for me at all. They were fitting me glasses on for an hour and a half and they cannot fit me with any better than these I have already got and it is the strain with doing close work and I have to appeal to come off the Welding. The Sister told me to see my own Dr tonight and see what he had to say about it. So I have been and he says if I carry on the strain will damage them more. So if I have to come off the job immediately and if they have not got another job for me I have to come out all together. Also if I have any trouble, I have to refer them to him. Believe me, I am <u>very very</u> upset about it because I don't want to leave the girls. In fact, I am going to risk it until Christmas I think. I feel so very upset for Mr Robinson too, because Enid is away poorly. That only leaves three of them if I chuck up. I am quite willing to carry on but I don't want my eyes to get any worse. My Doctors Certificate reads thus:

Miss Amy Brook is suffering from Myopic and Astigmatism and is unfit for Electric Welding (too much Eyestrain) 9/11/42

Signed G.I. Arnold

Our Evelyn was in the Doctor's. When I came out into the waiting room, Alec was with her. She has a Rupture, so she will have to go in the Infirmary for an Operation I expect. My mother has nearly gone mad over my eyes. I don't know what she will have to say when our Evelyn has to have an Operation. I am just having a good cry while I am trying to write this letter. I should have gone on A.R.P. duty but I have not the heart to go, I would much rather go and get a real good booze up. I am fed up.

Emily has done a bracket for me while I was away this afternoon, also one for herself. She is a real good sport and will do anything to help anybody. She said this afternoon, 'don't give up love, because I will always be ready to help you if you are behind'. I would be pleased to hear from you and let me have your version of the matter. I have not seen Sydney today I think he must be away because he usually spends a short while down Tank Alley. But he never comes in to look at us thank goodness. Are you hanging your Stocking up this year, if so, what are you expecting? The nurse gave Emily two strengthening tablets this morning and told her she was run down. I say Emily, Alice, and Ethel have had to go to a

Firewatching meeting at Hop's tonight, so I guess it will not be long before they are doing their bit.

I think I have given you all the news now, so I am waiting for an early reply, trusting you will not be annoyed over my job. But do not dismay because I have not thrown the towel in yet. I wonder what Fanny will have to say about it. Just let her know we are short staffed, will you, that might hasten her up a bit. Well, I will say goodnight and godbless and I will let you know when I come off the job if I do. New orders (give up smoking). Have I anything to live for do you think?

      Yours as before
        Love from,
          Aimee

IV Women and the War Machine: Letters from the 'Welding Wonders' of Huddersfield: Emily Jones, Ethel and John Kergon, Eleanor Hardcastle, Enid Hiley and Jenny

40 *A thank you letter from Emily*

Emily Castle (née Jones) was born in 1915, in Huddersfield. Her father worked as a lorry driver. She left school at 14 to work as a weaver in a mill. Aged 27, she was called up to work for Hopkinsons. She had met Norman, her husband to be, when he was 15 and she was 18. He was conscripted at 18, and was taken as a German prisoner-of-war in 1940.

Stafford Hill,
Kirkheaton,
Huddersfield

3 August 1942

Dear Miss Pearson
          How are you getting along, I suppose you will feel very lonely, or are you glad to be rid of us? I think we were quite a trial for you with our various troubles, and I don't think they are quite over, because Amy told me on Saturday, that Ethel had given John his ring back. But of course you know Ethel, she will probably be in his arms again by the time this reaches you. I suppose Agnes will be starting work this morning, presuming she has arrived back from Scotland intact. I am on nights this week and Amy is working until 7.00, so I shall not know until tonight, how things will turn out today. I am going up to Nellie's before I start work, and so are the rest of the girls. Incidentally, Nellie does not seem to get better like she ought to, she wants to start working but she is not really fit. I think she worries too much, and there is nothing like worry to pull one down, I know that from personal experience. I think it is mostly her mother, who by the way thinks Amy and I are two grand girls. You had better put her wise, and another thing I should just like to know why I need watching? I can assure you I have not committed any dark and deadly deeds nor slept underneath hedges, nor any that is wrong. How is Mrs Feather? we have not heard from her yet, she has let us down, I should just like to give her a piece

of my mind. Does Walter miss his little passion flower, or has he found another? Give my love to the Bull, but don't wave the red flag. Much as I enjoyed being over there I don't think I should like to be back. There's no place like home, I never thought so until now.

I have had two letters this week, and he seems to be alright. He [is] back on the land again, but says that his own back garden would suit him better. He also told me not to be a land girl. He doesn't know what I am really doing. Still it's better that way, he has enough worries as it is. I wonder if you still have our cards in the office, just Amy's and mine. They know nothing about them here, and they should have been in this last month. Would you please find out for us? I think that is all, so here's wishing you the best of luck, health and happiness,

Cheerio,
Emily

41–5   The courtship of Ethel and John

Ethel Kergon (née Richardson) married John Kergon, an engineer, in 1943.

10 Ark Hill,
Hillhouse,
Huddersfield

1 July 1942

Dear Miss Pearson,
     Before I go any further please let me introduce myself. I'm Ethel's 'John', by that I mean, John Kergon. No doubt you will be wondering what ever in the world I could have to say to you. Well, it is only because of what Ethel has told me about you, how you've been such a good friend to her, that I've taken the liberty of asking for a favour. Perhaps to you it will look like a piece of unheard of cheek, I suppose it is, but I'd do anything for Ethel. To get to the point though, I wonder if you remember having [a] conversation with Ethel, about an engagement ring, one she had seen, I think there was a green centre to it. I gathered, by the talk, that she would have liked it very much. Of course she did not say so, but I would like to give her a pleasant surprise, as well as a ring. I'm afraid I can only do this with your help. I wonder if you would be so kind as to go and buy it for me, I know that you would have to find out just where the shop was, without seeming too interested of course, and then there is the size. I enclose a ring that I'm fairly sure will fit, because I've seen Ethel wearing it on that finger. I suppose Ethel often wonders where that ring was lost, you see I've had the idea, as well as the ring, for quite some time now. The price, by the way, being £3.7.0 I believe, I think you will find enough for postage, and having it knocked down to fit. I wanted to give it to her at the holiday week, it would be a nice time, at least I think so. If you could possibly do this for me, I would be forever in your debt, but if you consider it just nerve, then I say, please forgive me. Until I know then, I wish to remain, in anticipation of being forever in your debt,
     Yours faithfully,
     John Kergon

42

10 Ark Hill,
Hillhouse,
Huddersfield

13 July 1942

Dear Val,

I don't quite know how to thank you for your kindness in going to all this trouble for me, or was it for Ethel? Please let me thank you ever so much. Whichever it was, you can be sure I'm very grateful, its such a nice little ring too. I made sure of having it cut to the required size by taking it straight to Town, they promised me faithfully to have it ready for Friday, so everything looks ready. I must admit I'm a bit scared though! I hope she hasn't guessed anything, for I've been dying to tell her all this weekend, and had to make up all sorts of excuses to cover up my mistakes! I never dreamed that one day I should be trying to ensnare a girl, I always thought that it was the other way round! Well, I mustn't take up any more of your time, so here is my thanks again, for everything, including the wishes for our future happiness, and may I add, that you too might find all the good things that go to make up a happy life time of matrimonial bliss, that is, if I'm not asking too much of life! I'm sorry I addressed you wrongly in my letter, but I will rectify the mistake this time, so once again, I thank you and close by wishing you the best of luck.

Yours faithfully,
John Kergon

43

c/o Miss Lewis,
2 Clifton Villas,
Queenshead,
Oswestry,
Shropshire

21 July 1942

Dear Val,

Everything went off as per plan and was Ethel pleased! I should say so, she nearly fell over herself in her excitement! It was a glorious start for our holidays, and up to now we are still having the time of our lives. Ethel, by the way, headed this but thought Dear Val too familiar! and wouldn't go any further and so, well here I am. I'd like to thank you once again for everything and I can assure you that we shall be very happy, we couldn't be any other, especially with friends like you! I popped the ? in the pictures on Saturday night, and 'boy' had I a sweat on! and had to mop my brow a bit first, and after you had told me to be cool and collected too! I forgot all that and everything else.

We intend going to Shrewsbury today and we shall be sending you a card from there as there is none to be had in this little spot where we're staying: one 'pubbe', one shop! Lovely place though, Ethel's mouth waters when she sees the plums on the trees! And the apples, pears, rasps, goose and every other kind of berry it seems, and all in one garden too. She bathed in the strawberry pie! I had perhaps better ring off now as I am being pestered by you know who, and here then I will wish you the best of luck and hand this over to Ethel, the best girl ever.

Yours faithfully,
John

44

Dear Miss Pearson,

(Excuse John being so familiar, but I haven't his cheek.) I would like to thank you dear, for being so kind, and doing what you did for John and I. I couldn't believe when he told me of the part you had taken in his little plan, and I must say you both carried your parts off well, never even a suggestion of anything out of the ordinary going off, and until he showed me the letters you had sent him, I found it hard to believe. We are having a glorious time down here, and the weather has been swell so far. I couldn't send you a card, because the one and only shop around these parts, when we enquired about some, hadn't seemed to have heard of such things as post cards. I suppose the last one was sold 18 . . . Anyway it is quite the most loveliest country side I have seen, what a contrast to Coleridge Rd. All the same, I was sorry to leave good old Sheffield, and I only wish that if I have to leave all this next week, that I was coming back to Welding Rods, for it will break my heart starting at Hopkinson. But there, talking about work in a spot like this, with the sun shining glorious and John urging me to hurry up and go out with him. I haven't heard from the girls yet, but I'm not surprised, I've never seen a post man since Friday. I will say Cheerio now dear, and thanks once again, hoping to see you very soon,

     Love,

       Ethel

45

> 57 Belle Vue Cres,
> Sheepridge,
> Huddersfield

> Tuesday [August 1942]

Dear Val,

Before I say anything, please let me thank you for giving me this privilege of using your first name when writing to you.

Well dear, how are you going on now that you haven't your eight welding wonders to pester you? But even yet I hear you keep having flying visits from the girls. Don't be surprised if we all don't pop over one of these days because, for all the good we are doing here, we may just as well be at home. I haven't lifted my hands to work all this week so far, I asked for another job as my other was finished, at 8.45 on Monday. They still haven't brought me anything to do, I just get the answer on enquiring 'you're all right, what are you bothering for.' I am speaking for myself, but the rest of the mob are equally as badly off. The days seem like months.

Well, before I leave the subject of work, I must tell you what happened to Fanny this afternoon, who by the way hangs out, (I can't say works) alongside of me. One of the lads whispered to me he would have her (Fanny) on a little, so he asked if she would go to the stores for him, and Fan being the kind soul she is, gladly consented to do so. What he told her to fetch was a '$\frac{1}{2}$' putting on tool, female, and of course this seemed quite logic to unsuspecting Fanny, so off she trots to the stores and finally has the whole machine shop in tears of laughter. She never alters does she? But she's a good sort and good fun.

I am staying in this evening to catch up with my mail, for I have four letters to answer, and I knew the only way to do this was have a night off. It is the first night I have stayed in since I came home, for if I haven't been with John, I have been with the girls. I arranged to meet Jenny on Sunday but on arriving ten minutes late (as usual) and not finding her there I went back home. However I learned on Monday that she had waited until half an hour had passed, but had meanwhile taken a walk around so I missed her. You can guess she was rather wild about it, and said Fanny and I ought to get together. John has kept asking me if I had written to you, but as I told him, I couldn't do much when he was taking up all my time.

We still have our little quarrels but they never seem to last more than a few hours. The reason, I think, is because we neither of us like to admit we are wrong in our own points of view. Still that doesn't stop us from loving each other, and the best of it is, it seems to get more instead of less as the days roll by. No kidding though, I think that he and I seem to have found what everyone is seeking, but without doubt we have lots to learn yet, in regards to giving and taking.

Did you know dear that my mother was really put up about our engagement, and was quiet a while before she spoke to John. But I think she is coming round now, I hope so because I would hate to hurt Mum, she's such a grand person really. I suppose it was rather a shock to her hearing the news John broke to her.

I do hope it won't be long, Val dear, before you come to Huddersfield. We will have a swell time, because we are already discussing the plans for your welfare.

How is your Dad keeping? Well, I hope, and please remember me to him will you, also the rest of the folks. How's 'Bull', still as boring as ever I suppose. And now, I shall have to bring my letter to a close, so I'll say Cheerio, and lots of love dear,

Yours,

Ethel

P.S. I mustn't forget that John sends his love too. This is so important as I have had it drilled into me.

46–50   Nellie's troubles

Nellie was an only daughter. Her father had died by the time she was called up.

> 26 Springfield Rd,
> Birkby,
> Hudds

> 7 July 1942

Dear Miss Pearson,
          I hope you don't mind not turning up Monday.[83] When I arrived home Friday Night, Mother was bed-fast, has been all week. I was annoyed, she said that I would be upset if she had sent word. However will come Tuesday without fail.
          Wish 'Emmerlieeeeee', as Agnes ('Fanny') calls her, 'Many Happy Returns' and hope you all have a jolly time. I shall be thinking about you all, as I am 'Smoothing away with a soothing iron' after Monday's wash-day.
          I wonder if you would ask one of the Girls to bring the Umbrella, (hung up in the Wardrobe) down to the works, as I shall have to take it to Rotherham. It's Sidney's sister's. Did you have a nice weekend Miss Pearson? I hope you did.
          I told you that an enemy was in your Tea-Cup, one day, but I think it 'hopped' into mine, for Sidney and I had a right talk starting in the train, so that was the reason he made for the other carriage (tell the girls). They were pulling my leg. That is the reason he has been quiet, his Cousin has been talking. However will tell you when we meet.
          We have had a glorious weekend together, and would not leave me till Sunday Morning. I mean under the circumstances we could not leave Mother, (but we knew where she was) (bad girl Nellie).
          Well dear, I hope I have not bored you, also I do hope you don't mind me having Monday off, but she will be downstairs, and shall feel easier then.
          Thanking you once again
                    Wishing you everything of the Best,
                              Yours Sincerely,
                                        Nellie

---

[83] This letter was written while she was still in training at Welding Rods.

47

26 Springfield Rd,
Birkby,
Hudds

1 August 1942

Dear Miss Pearson,

I am very sorry that I have 'let you down' again so suddenly, but I ought to have told you last week, that I did not feel well. But with all the 'upset' among the girls, and one thing and another, I felt you had quite enough to think about.

Well Miss Pearson, I had to go to the Doctor's Saturday. My eyes were sore, could not see out of one, my body and arms are one mass of spots, it starts irritating at nights cannot sleep, she told me I was run down to the bottom. Am sending the Dr. Certificate for you to see, will be obliged if you would return it as soon as possible, for insurance.

Yours, truly.
Nellie

48

26 Springfield Rd,
Birkby,
Hudds

[August 1942]

Dear Miss Pearson,
        Am writing in ink, but I am another step higher, sitting in
the room now, and just walked down the street, felt grand.
        Received your most charming letters, did me good I can
tell you. I laughed at the sleeping out bit. We ought to have been
playing 'consequences', would have pulled your leg.
        Do you know dear, I received the flowers on my Birthday?
What a pleasant surprise, people that came to see me, said 'How
lovely', smell, smell, till I thought there won't be any roses left and
no smell.
        Of course the 'twins' had to take a flower.[84] They have been
everyday, shall miss them next week. Received letters from the girls.
If Fanny does not go anywhere next week, will write and ask her
to come, she does want to see me she says.
        Sid's Mother would like me to go when I feel stronger and
have a few days, but shall not sleep under the hedge. (Now then
Nellie, none of that.) So now dear I must close, thanking you again
for your kindness, and will write again to you. Do remember me
to the 'Miss A.T.S.' and will tell her very quickly, when I do the
'Big Thing'.
        With Best Wishes
                yours sincerely,
                        Nellie

P.S. Alice 'old Faithful' has just called, but to my dismay I thought
I was receiving my 'Holiday with Pay'. She laughed when she saw
my face, or shall I say 'Mug drop', when she hadn't it. What about,
Madam Pearson, aren't I entitled to it, or can't I 'HAVE IT'?
        Something else now.
                Cheerio,
                        Nell

---

[84] Amy and Emily.

49

26 Springfield Rd,
Birkby,
Hudds

[August 1942]

Dear Miss Pearson,

Received your nice welcome letter, it did cheer me up. I'm afraid mine is going to be miserable. Have had too many visitors this weekend. When the Doctor saw me she said – 'My word dear, you are done up' and I did feel it too.

I cannot go away yet, in fact she won't let me go out. If I do, straight to visit her and back again.

Oh Miss Pearson, am worried to death, what with my work, and then had another row with Mother, that has put me back, it's over Sid again. (But if you feel like writing dear, don't mention the row with Ma, she reads all my letters.) His People came and brought me eggs, Strawberries, and butter, and then my Ma said I made more of them than her. 'I wish I was dead, out of the way,' she said. If Jenny had the worry I have, she would need to grouse to Mr Pearson and Mr Wright.

Mother is complaining now of a pain catching her in her back. That's where I feel it being the only one. The Unemployment Place ought never to have sent for me, leaving a woman of 72, the[re] are never two days alike. The Dr says it's worry that's brought me down like this, and then the other affair.

However I must not bore you with my troubles. How is your Dad and Mother? Kindly remember me to them. I only wish I had my Father, things would have been different.

Did you have a nice weekend? I hope so.

So now I will close. If you have not time, dear, don't write, I know you have plenty to do. But all the same, shall be awfully delighted.

Yours Sincerely,
Nellie

50

26 Springfield Rd,
Birkby,
Hudds

3 September 1942

Dear Miss Pearson,
No doubt you will think I have forgotten but not likely
dear. Will tell you the reason I am so long in writing. Well, first of
all I got quite alright again, only soon tired (that's nothing) so I went
to see Mar-Flet[85] and she said, there was nothing for me to do, would
I like another week, — took it, and cleaned down from top to
bottom so that's off my mind.
Went to Hops last Monday and am on a Bogey-Machine,
and it's like your Dad says, they don't know what the devil they are
doing. This machine I'm on smooths off.[86] Now we have at times
smoothed too much. Next gets tested, they all talk again, makes it
too little, then, decide to send a man down to London. Really, I
don't think they know what to do. Same with drilling holes in the
plates, they were too small. I like it, it's interesting, you have plenty
of Knobs to turn and push in, and I keep saying 'Harry it is stiff you
can you help me', he replies 'what is' then we laugh. (Dirty mind
you have, Nellie.) How are you Dear and Boy Friend, any more
'Dirty Stop Outs', (cheeky) aren't I?
I went over to Fanny, to see how she was, but was out, and
her Mother was just going to have her Bath, (she says), going to
London. But Agnes was still poorly.
Amy had all of us up to their house Tuesday Night. We
had a nice evening's Sing Song, in fact her brother politely wanted
to know if it was the 'Siren of the All Clear'? Guess what a row
we made.
How is your Mum and Dad? Remember me to them, and
heaps of Love to you dear. Forgive me for not writing earlier. Have
you had the Sirens? We were up last Thursday, but Aunty was over
for a few weeks rest, from Sunderland. They have been in it awful,
her House was hit, she looks ill. However she has gone back.
So now I will close.
Cheerio yours sincerely,
Nellie xx

[85] Mrs Marflit.
[86] Mills off the extra slag.

51–2 *Jenny gets out of welding*

Jenny was married when she was called up. She only worked at Hopkinsons for a few weeks. She was discharged because of 'impertinence to the manager' because she asked him on the shopfloor whether she could leave the job.

76, Upper Brow Rd,
Paddock,
Huddersfield

4 August 1942

My Dear Miss Pearson,
    I hope you haven't forgotten who I am, though I wouldn't be surprised as it has taken me a long time to write to you, hasn't it? You will forgive me?
    No doubt the other girls have told just what we all think of Hopkinsons, so I wont go into detail about it. All I can say is I think it is a lousy trick they are playing on us.[87] Mr Wright has never spoken to us at all, except to say hello once when Mr Pearson was there.[88]
    Ethel and I went along to the place where we are supposed to start welding and found the place still in a state of chaos. There are eight machines and eight turn-tables all lined up along the wall just as they were the day we arrived here. So what?
    Ethel, Agnes and I have been sitting together for about a week doing a spot of painting. I wish you could have seen us. Anyway our boss Mr Brooks came along this afternoon and put Agnes in charge of a machine. It is set up by a man and all she has to do is sit and watch it for about half an hour, then it stops automatically. It's hard work. Well, we went along to see how she was going on and Mr Brooks caught us and Oh! Boy what language, did he swear telling us to get back where we came from.[89]
    Well, I haven't time to write anymore just now as I have some washing to do as the laundry is on holiday, so Cheerio.
    Lots of Luck and Best Wishes,
        Jenny xxx

[87] Presumably the long delay in beginning work welding, rather than more menial jobs. They were also not being paid what they'd expected.
[88] Valentine's father appears to have visited Hopkinsons from time to time, probably on business as the supplier of welding material.
[89] See Agnes's version of this in Letter 11.

52

76, Upper Brow Rd,
Paddock, Hudds

23 August 1942

My Dear Miss Pearson,
      Thanks for your very enjoyable letter. Yes they are my sandals
and I left them by accident. If you can remember, would you like
to bring them <u>when</u> you come to Hops?
      We had quite a shock this week. We were told we may be
welding by Monday. But alas and alack, it is the usual nazi-report.
      Anyway there is one booth up and do they look funny. The
machine hasn't been coupled up yet or I should ask them if I could
practise a bit as I haven't got a job. I didn't know it was such hard
work doing nothing. I only did about 20 mins work on Sat morning.
By the way, I'm working in the same room as Alice, Enid and Emily.
We see Amy each morning, she always looks tired out and she hasn't
been too well this last week, it's her tummy. I think.
      We have a terrible time with the fellows they tease us
awful. Enid has a new name now. Daphne Squeaker, because they
say she squeaks when she gets mad.
      I'm afraid I haven't got any news to tell you. Everything is
so dull at work and I don't go out in the black out if I can help it.
      Give my regards to Mr Pearson and to yourself.
            Lots of Luck.
                  Yours with love.
                        Jenny

53   *The final letter from Enid*

55 Hangingstone Rd,
Berry Brow,
Hudds

11 October 1942

Dear Miss Pearson,

Thank you so much for your letter, it was lovely to hear from you. I seem to have got out of the habit of writing since I left Sheffield. Of course nothing worth recording ever happens here in Huddersfield.

Amy and I visited Agnes shortly after your visit to Hops, and we hadn't been there long when Fanny presented me with my note book, and also an old one of Emily's, so I shan't have to get anyone else's now.[90] I'm sorry to have had you searching for it, but perhaps it has kept you from worse things.

The girls and myself are still getting along fine with the welding &, from what I can gather, Mr Pearson was quite pleased with us on his round of inspection last week.

Would you believe it (our Sydney) actually came and asked me how I liked being on exhibition, (& was I mad).[91] I promptly answered that I had been on exhibition before, meaning, of course, our interview in his office. He said 'Oh I'm sorry' and walked away. After that I thought, well perhaps I was a bit rude, so I apologised, and what do you think he said? He told me that he never thought a lady rude as it was their prerogative. I was at sea as to what that meant, so answered 'oh', and on looking it up saw that it meant 'an exclusive or peculiar privilege'. Isn't he a devil? You ought to hear the names he gets, they are real snorters.

Ethel found her ring again, but there was a stone missing, so she is having it repaired. She has been out with a boy that works at Hops since then. I'm afraid there will be a murder if John gets to know.

Emily is now welding the little top parts on the brackets and says it's a terrible job. So we are going to take it in turns and believe me, Ethel used some language last week, so what will happen when it's her turn, heaven alone knows.

Amy is still as lively as ever and runs round in circles trying to get her work done quickly. The other day Mr Robinson passed

---

[90] Possibly her technical notes from the course at Welding Rods.
[91] Sydney Wright, the boss of Hopkinsons.

her cubicle and he said he thought there must be a dozen people in at least and on looking found there was only our little 'Aimeeee' swearing away and carrying on 'something shocking' and just imagine Amy's horror when she heard later in the day that Mr R was a Parson's son.

We also have been given our fire-watchers' forms and Mrs Marflett says it will only be very seldom that we are on duty, as there are so many girls here. We are only expected to fire-watch from 7 till 9 in the evening as they have a night shift here all night. Mrs Muffet, 'as all the men call her', is still on the war path. She prowls round in the most unexpected places. On Friday Emily went to the place to spend a penny and the door of the one she was in had no catch, but everyone understands that when a door is closed that the place is occupied. She had just got prepared when (Wham!) went the door and behold Mrs M. stood there, so of course the door went (wham!) the other way. But hardly was the position reversed when Mrs M. says 'Is there only one of you in there' and Emily answered 'How many does it take to do this job?' So now we are all in bad books again. But who cares? We don't.

They haven't got our tables fixed up yet, but with Emily being on another job we are kept at it now.

When Mr Pearson was round the other day, one of us must have given Mr Wright a flash and he came in with both his eyes bunged up the next day. He came straight down to the shop and had some more curtains fixed over the spaces of others, so perhaps he knows what it feels like now.

Cyril and I are going housekeeping tonight. Some friends of ours, who haven't been married long, keep lending us their key to get some practice, they say. The last time we went, Frank and Phil came back and were surprised to find us playing Monopoly. I wonder what they expected?

There isn't much to tell you so I will close now, hoping to see you soon.

Lots of Love,
Enid

P.S. It was Agnes that was fascinated with Walter's bald head and not me. I have quite enough to do looking after one that is nearly bald. Perhaps it will turn me bald if welding doesn't burn it off. Cheerio

Epilogue: Whose Story? A History Told Through Letters

Valentine did more than save the letters. Only months after receiving them, she sent them to a social research organisation, Mass-Observation. The organisation was unique. Established five years earlier in 1937, its founders, the anthropologist Tom Harrisson, journalist Charles Madge and documentary film-maker Humphrey Jennings, aimed to create a record of everyday life, 'an anthropology of ourselves'. Their idea was in many ways ahead of its time, and their methods were even more iconoclastic. They invited people to become 'Mass-Observers' and send in their observations of such everyday topics as hygiene, sex in Blackpool and what people did on Sundays, as well as current affairs. They welcomed the subjective and the idiosyncratic. One of the original researchers scrawled on the bundle of welders' letters, 'Fascinating Stuff'.

But Mass-Observation clearly also had its own biases, recognised and unrecognised. Most of its 'observers' as well as its directors, were middle or upper class, and most of the 'observed' were working class. Furthermore, its interest in 'ordinary' people attracted the wartime Ministry of Information, which employed it to monitor morale and public opinion. While the directors certainly made use of this to try to influence government opinion in progressive ways, their wartime job points up how delicate the distinction is between representing and controlling people through recording their lives.

This delicate balance had a particular twist in the case of the welders' letters. For Valentine, who had volunteered to be a 'Mass-Observer' in 1939, had sent them in without telling her correspondents. Since the letters belonged to her, she was within her legal rights to do so.[64] But was she right to turn private documents into public information without their authors' knowledge?

Letters since the seventeenth century have been published without authorial consent, celebrated as 'stolen' postbags that offer the thrill

---

* The notes for the Epilogue are on pages 167–9.

of a glimpse into the private lives of unknowing subjects. But it is interesting that these have typically been women's letters, for women, even of the aristocracy, have historically been considered unworthy of the rights of true 'authors'. Seen as 'scribblers' instead, their letter writing has often been praised, but in the double-edged terms of 'spontaneity' and 'artlessness'. Arguably, Valentine's act was a parallel kind of upper-middle-class disregard for working-class authorship. But, at the same time, her own and the Archive's interest in the letters clearly reflected an excitingly democratic conception of what constituted both culture and the means by which it could be recorded.

This book cannot escape these tensions. Inevitably, Valentine has left the public reader not only a legacy of some 'fascinating stuff', but in the position of reading what was not originally intended for our eyes. But this, of course, is part of why the letters tell a good story. Refreshingly free of wartime propagandic jargon, they tell of an unofficial and sometimes taboo war. They show us squabbles, ambitions, jokes and differences, rather than the patriotic homogeneity that flattens so much of even the personal forms of wartime writing.

The collected form of the letters itself represents a distortion of the writers' original intentions. Yet, again, it is precisely the fact that we have all their different versions of the same events that makes them interesting to the public reader. A helpful context for thinking about this is Patricia Spacks's argument that the public reading of private letters has long been characterised by a kind of literary voyeurism. Far from condemning this, she sees it as an important recognition of the creative potential of a usually denigrated genre. Publication turns writers into characters, or in her terms, gossipees as well as gossipers (Spacks 1986: 65–91). I will show briefly how this works in terms of this collection before taking up the question of the authority of the letter writers, of Valentine and of myself as editor.

In the Penistone letters, the incident of Joan's wedding is a nodal point: we learn from Dorothy and Joan of the difficulties planning around her fiancé's tenuous leave; the lack of ingredients for the cake; and then afterwards, from Joan, that 'Violet and Helena got canned on Saturday at the wedding'. The tensions within the group are suggested in Violet's contrasting account, in which she tells us, 'Dot was disgusted at us and said we let the welders down.' This is modulated, however, by Dorothy's later comment that 'Joan's husband has gone to Northern Ireland and Joan and I are having a good time, I can't believe she's married yet.' In the Huddersfield community's letters, Agnes's pregnancy and the engagement of Ethel and John Kergon become unifying plots. John's letters serve as a foil to the different attitude and registers of the women, and draw us further into their perspectives as others comment on the affair. Amy is unimpressed: 'Well the ring does not appeal to me at all, I don't know what you think about it it strikes me she had been romancing again I don't know whatever John carries on for her like he does' (Letter 21). And: 'About the ring I am disgusted with Ethel, I think if she goes away with him and then carries on as before, she is a downright rotter' (Letter 22). Emily's account is kinder:

> Amy told me on Saturday, that Ethel had given John his ring back, but of course you know Ethel, she will probably be in his arms again by the time this reaches you. (Letter 40)

I cannot help but wonder if John's trepidation about trying to 'ensnare' his girl was justified – after the drama in which Ethel lost and found the ring, Enid claims in a later letter that Ethel is seeing someone behind John's back:

> Ethel found her ring again but there was a stone missing so she is having it repaired, she has been out with a boy that works at Hops since then, I'm afraid there will be a murder if John gets to know. (Letter 53)

But Ethel then resolves the story for us, in what now reads as a romance satirised by an actively scribbling community in the best epistolary tradition:

> We still have our little quarrell's but they never seem to last more than a few hour's. The reason I think is because we neither of us like to admit we are wrong in our own point's of view. Still that does'nt stop us from loving each other, and the best of it is, it seems to get more instead of less as the day's roll by. No kidding though, I think that he and I seem to have found what every one is seeking, but without doubt we have lot's to learn yet, in regards to giving and taking.
>   Did you know dear that my mother was really put up about our engagement, and was quiet a while before she spoke to John, but I think she is coming round now, I hope so because I would hate to hurt Mum, she's such a grand person realy, I suppose it was rather a shock to her hearing the news John broke to her. (Letter 45)

In this overlapping of individual tales, a tenuous narrative structure emerges which can encompass the group perspectives. This unity is what coaxes the collection towards a literary structure, a proto-epistolary novel. But of course, a letter collection is much more fragmented and disrupted than a novel or even an autobiography. Its unity is one that is buffeted by social hazards whose micro-scale – mother's opposition, others' cynicism – implies the everyday, relentless nature of the writers' struggle with sexual destiny.

Clearly these are personal letters whose appeal is this human scale. But reading all of these stories together asserts the full force of the women's preoccupation with this destiny, worked through at the nervous level of an anticipatory rather than retrospective unfolding of events. Of course, the consistent theme of sexual and private drama, as we have seen, is in part the reflection of Valentine's interests. It is her eye, perhaps, that unifies, as the repeated reference to her own 'hedgebottoming' episode implies. But the lack of authorial narrator is symbolic. In other words, the very fact that the narrative is embedded, unfinished, that there is a kind of tension between the story and its breakdown, becomes representative of the characters' engagement with a harder history. There is none of the promised transcendence of the conscious autobiographer, but an emerging story whose very unconsciousness can give both literary effect and historical import. In my view, this effect explains and justifies the publication of private letters, and indeed, I consider that the special interest of letter collections is too often neglected.

But acknowledging the authorial rights of letter writers remains a difficult issue. As we have seen, this is particularly so in this case, given that these writers did not know their letters had been saved, nor the nature of the organisation where the letters were kept. It was this that made it crucial to try to talk to the surviving women, not only to discuss copyright, but their views on the letters' preservation, on Valentine, and on the way that they would be represented if the letters were to be published. So, in May 1994, I set off for Huddersfield.

I was directed by Dorothy Sheridan, who works as the Archivist for what has become the Mass-Observation Archive.[65] With Penny Summerfield, she had already traced the surviving writers in 1985. It was then, 43 years after the women had written their letters, that they discovered what Valentine had done. Penny Summerfield had interviewed Agnes, Emily, Amy and Helena in 1989 and they, with Ethel, John and Enid, all agreed to publication. But the project had foundered through lack of funding. By the time I interviewed them,

five years later, while enthusiastic about the project as a whole, they
questioned why the public would be interested in their letters, and
sometimes whether indeed the public or I *should* be interested.

In my interviews with Agnes, Ethel and John, Emily and Alice
(the last did not write any letters but was part of the Huddersfield
group), and Dorothy and Joan from Penistone, we discussed these
questions, alongside their war experiences and subsequent life
histories. Over cups of tea and the erratic hum of the tape recorder,
they told me how they felt about being confronted with forgotten
letters written in their youth. Especially tricky, but interesting, was
the fact that, in order for them to have the same knowledge as an
editor or public reader, they had to read *each other's* letters, which
clearly involved their relationships with each other, now as well as
then. From these meetings, two central points emerged. The first
was that there was a big difference between memory and letter,
suggesting that the interviews had produced their own versions of
events, following a genre of retrospect and idealisation of the past.
The second took us back to the letters themselves as creative texts.

First, I will consider the difference between memory and letter.
The women talked about their work as welders as exceptional,
something neither sought for nor lasting. Yet their letters, as we have
seen, offered a more permanent and sometimes more positive view
of the job. They talked about their decision to leave, marry, have
a family. But, on questioning, they described being demoted as the
men came back. The welders at David Brown were, once again,
put on core-making. At Hopkinsons, they were moved to other parts
of the factory, or they left, to have children or for health reasons.
The clearest example of a contrast between the letters and interview
was Amy's response to Penny's question 'Did you ever want to weld
again?' Her reply: 'Oh no, no way. I wanted an easy job.'[66] But Amy
in fact had attempted to continue welding after the war, enrolling
on a City and Guilds course at a local college. Her letters repeatedly
suggest that this was the result of a very personal ambition:

I guess at this moment you will be enjoying a cuddley woodly
with G I have not seen Chick nor heard from him since the Tuesday
you was at Hops I cannot tell what has happened what with the
worry over him and then Fanny [Agnes] I am just about in a trance
so you must please excuse all mistakes and writing because I am
writing this any style. I am looking forward to seeing you again
before long because I might not live very long now I am fixed
to a welding plant all day long. I have already developed a shocking

cold but hope it does not last long, because I cannot have any
Rum to cure it. I have turned good all at once I am teetotal and
dont swear, from now on, and I now say my prayers every night
that is owing to my Welding, I really am taking the job serious
and I am going to stick at it until I am as good as you, and then
is the time to fly my kyte and have a good time, until then I am
a good girl, unless I see you in the meantime and then maybe I
would soften for a few drinks. (Letter 31)

Amy left her welding course after a few months. Perhaps, without
the company of other women and Val, out of the context of the
war effort, it was too difficult to prove that welding was not a
'man's job'. 'Taking the job serious' for a woman, as is clear from
the above, involves hazarding with feminine virtue. It is unsurprising
that none of the women continued welding, even Val, who did try,
but was told that she could not do the heavy lifting and oxyacetylene
welding needed in the small village context, where she was then living.
But the letters are a reminder of the ambitions that they once had
in that direction.

Further dramatic disparities between memories and the letters
emerged in my interviews. Ethel was more than surprised to discover
the allegations that she had been going out with another boy. Agnes
had had no idea that Dorothy from Penistone, whom she had not
seen since she was a child, had written about her to Valentine, and
was more shocked to read of her own dramatic escapades with
blue-eyed Eddie, the airman, and her attempts to terminate the
pregnancy. Emily, who did not have very good memories of
Valentine, claimed that the typescript of the chatty, personal letter
wasn't hers, for she had only 'written a thank you letter'.[67] Indeed,
all of them, except for Agnes, were somewhat surprised at the
apparent interest they had had in their former trainer, whom now
they thought little about, in contrast to her own highly detailed and
individualised portraits of her students.

These disparities were, in part, the differences between perceptions
in old age and in youth. Reminiscence inherently tends to structure
life as coherent and consecutive, a story tending towards a resolving
closure. But, while this is interesting enough, it would be wrong to
attribute their different perceptions solely to the imaginative patterns
of memory. Rather, they were the result of reminiscence in interview
with Penny or me. In other words, these were responses within that
particular social context, a conversation between white English
women of different generations, in which I relished their memories

as a respectful granddaughter, but also enjoyed their letters as a young woman like they had been when they wrote, steering between work, love and sexuality.[68] It was perhaps unsurprising that I formed a particular friendship with Agnes. Still the performer, she was thrilled with the idea of publishing the letters, and in the same way thrived on interviews, reading me her occasional poetry which was written, like letters, for a particular reader, 'to give them a message'.[69] As she had been interested in Valentine, so she was interested in me.

My identification with Valentine was perhaps the most important element in the interview process. This was in part simply because she was the addressee of the letters and, as I have said, this immediately gave me her overview. Structurally she is the individual in relation to the writers as the group. But, second, my relationship to them as middle-class researcher to working-class interviewee, a largely absent but interpretative presence, replicated the original terms of letter writing to Valentine. In my view, this made for a relationship that was both creative and limiting in similar ways, as our different experiences of class played across common interests as women.

My interviews with Valentine herself, surrounded by Siamese cats and Balinese batiks, underlined my own process of identification. My wish to write about and publish the letters could not help but merge with her delight that her long-forgotten consecration of the letters to Mass-Observation had borne fruit. Her view of the women as 'characters' was close to my construction of a story through letters. Describing the arrival of the Huddersfield group in Sheffield, she said:

> VM: They were there for a long time, and so I got to know them very well, and they told me their troubles and all about their families and their relations.
> MJ: Why do you think they told you all their troubles?
> VP: Well, for one thing, I'm a good listener, ha, ha, and also, I was interested. You know I'm interested in people, and all their little problems, and why they function like they do. Well, I'm interested in psychology and what makes people do this and that. And if you're interested, people like to talk to you don't they?

All this suggested the ways that interviews themselves are genres, creating their own stories not only out of memory, but relationship.[70] But if this seemed to edge towards re-establishing the letters as the objective 'evidence' of the past against the subjective projections of the present, it was undermined by the story of Amy.

Amy had told Penny in 1989 that she had no memories of Chick, Harry or any of the wartime romances described with such gaiety in her letters. This was perhaps unsurprising, forty-three years and a marriage later. I was not able to interview Amy herself, since she had died in 1990. However, at a reunion tea party, Alice, Agnes, Ethel and Emily also assured me that Amy certainly never had such boyfriends, or indeed any boyfriends at all during the war. They talked about her sober and chaste energy, commenting, indeed, that this explained her dislike of Ethel's 'romancing'. 'She was quite school-marmish', Ethel told me. What did this mean for her letters? Agnes read aloud incriminating passages. They roared with laughter when Amy signed off 'I must go and prepare to meet my lover!' In their view, Amy was clearly exaggerating, if not fantasising, perhaps taking advantage of her absent reader to make up a more glamorous self. In my view, it hardly mattered whether the five boyfriends were fictional or not. The point was that Amy had really made use of the correspondence to 'write' a self who would have been censored by her family and friends.

The tea party showed the constructive nature of memory. But it also showed, once again, the constructive nature of writing, so obvious in the letter where the self is projected for a particular and known reader. Indeed, the research brought out the continuities between oral history interview and the letter as plural and dialogic forms of creation.

This book, too, is clearly a joint effort, a meld of different, but mutually dependent, genres. And in this story, all of us – writers, editors, archivist, historians – have both gained and lost authority. The writers were, and are, pleased to see their letters published, but have had to trust me as editor. At the same time, my confident overview as 'public' reader has disintegrated as the controls of reading in the abstract fell apart through meeting the authors. Through those meetings, life and writing came closer, aptly signalled by me becoming part of the correspondence between Valentine and Agnes – their 'character' – as well as beginning my own correspondence with them.[71] On another level, the contrast between letter and reminiscence in interview necessarily underlines the gap between text and life, and the problematic nature of all authority.

What, then, of the practical decisions involved in editing? The collection was tricky to edit, neither fitting a biographical nor anthological structure. I chose to divide the letters by writer, within an overall chronology, in part to create comprehensibility out of twelve writers of short letters, but also to bring out the distinctiveness of each voice in the interests of enhancing their authority.[72] For the same reason I have regularised most of the spelling, grammar and layout. On the other hand, I have gone for a more flowery kind of 'reader-friendliness' in giving the letters 'captions' and photographs which show what they did rather than who they were. Their own photographs of the period were less reproducible and did not show them at work.

Perhaps the most testing of all editorial interventions is the ending of a correspondence. Even where the stories are multiple, as here, the reader craves to know 'what happened' to the protagonists. The question of the 'ending', in fact, reveals most clearly the aesthetic at stake in editing, not only as a question of reading pleasure but ideological meaning. In this case, my own editorial treatment suggests a genre that has its own 'romance' elements: a carnivalesque tale of anti-heroines brought into proto-sisterhood through the novelty of welding. Yet, as I have suggested, this may owe as much to middle-class (women's) fantasies about working-class women's self-representations as it does to the ideals of contemporary feminism or socialism. My aim has been to bring out the auto/biographical dimensions of the letters as an unfolding plot of self, crosshatched not only by the relationship with Valentine but by the wider historical events that determined the writers' lives. But the group story of sexual struggle that I have described is *my* re/construction, not the women's, created out of the pointillist nature of the epistolary self.

Helena married in 1946. She reverted to core-making that year and left Brown's in 1948 when she became pregnant. She had three children. Her husband went back to moulding in various foundries, after being in the Royal Air Force, but then received a state scholarship to Balliol College, Oxford as a mature student. He eventually worked as head of an adult education centre. Helena kept in touch with Violet.

Dorothy married in 1947. She had reverted to core-making in 1946 and left Brown's in 1949 when she became pregnant. She had two children. She became a qualified caterer and head cook in a comprehensive school kitchen until her retirement, at age 65.

Joan lived through her husband's difficult adjustment to civilian life on returning from the Royal Air Force in 1945. She had a child in 1948 and worked at various jobs including rent collecting and for Empire Stores. She and Dorothy are still good friends.

Violet married Arnold Jessop in 1945 and left Brown's to have a child. She returned to Brown's in 1953 as a crane driver and left for health reasons in 1957. She died c.1994. No more information is known.

Emily left Hopkinsons in 1945, the minute she heard her fiancé Norman was back. They married that year. Mr Robinson, their supervisor at Hopkinsons, suggested that she take a City and Guilds training course in welding but she refused the offer. She stopped paid work when her daughter was born in 1947. She kept in touch with Amy.

Alice stayed on at Hopkinsons until she retired at the age of 60, moving from welding to the orders and post department. She lived at home with her parents, and then brother, until moving into a retirement home.

Ethel married John in 1943. She worked briefly in the stores section of Hopkinsons, before starting a family. John continued to work as an engineer. She still wears the ring he bought her with Valentine's help.

Enid married Cyril. She did not keep in contact with the other women. She died in 1986.

Nellie stopped welding in 1943 due to ill health. She moved to Whitley Bay, where she lived with a woman friend with whom she had worked at Hopkinsons, until her death in 1986.

It has been impossible to trace Jenny.

Agnes stayed on at Hopkinsons, with many breaks due to illness, until 1945. Jack returned from the Navy to a job as an engineer. They had a son in 1947. She struggled with ill health for the rest of her life. She kept in touch with Amy and wrote to Valentine until her death in 1995.

Amy enrolled on a City and Guilds certificate course in welding, but left after a few months, to work briefly as a waitress for Mr and Mrs Robinson in their boarding house in Scarborough, then as a clerk at ICI, and at Holroyd's dry cleaners. She eventually worked as a supervisor at David Brown Tractors.[73] She married William Hargate aged 44, another Hopkinsons' employee. She kept in touch with Agnes and Emily and wrote to Valentine until her death in 1990.

Valentine emigrated with Gottfried in 1947 to British Columbia, Canada. They bought a fruit farm on the edge of a remote lake in the Canadian Rockies, and worked as subsistence farmers. Her parents emigrated to live near them in 1948. She had no children, preferring to raise Siamese cats, Afghan hounds, llamas and peacocks. She did not return to England until 1984, when she visited Agnes and Amy in Huddersfield.

Amy to Valentine:

Late 1985

I wonder how the Archivist is getting on I have not had any more news from her so I suppose her and her friend will be getting it all together all those choice letters of mine will be under the hammer now, I would love to read them no doubt I would derive a lot of pleasure reading them today, you so and so. I was good at letter writing those days, but not now . . .

Valentine to Agnes:

3 July 1995

Dearest Agnes,
 A lot has happened since I last wrote. In order of happening – Margaretta Jolly phoned . . . it was decided she would come in June and stay from Friday till Monday . . . She brought transcripts of all the letters, and the interviews by Penny Singleton.[74] So while I read all of those; she read your and Aimy's letters that you've sent to me here – then she did 6 hours interviewing me on tape – Your ears must have been red hot.
 It was great talking about those times again, in fact we spent most of the weekend on the subject . . . Your letters were so descriptive and full of life – I really enjoyed reading them again – Of course John's letter about buying the engagement ring was a high point (Ethel having told him exactly how much it cost) and me finding out from you girls which one it was etc: then John's joyous account in his next letter of her delight, and accepting him on the spot. A bit later, one of your letters announces that they've had a row and shes given it him back – But she'll probably change her mind – which of course, she did –
 I had forgotten about your trip to visit Jack in Scotland, and the soldiers! We had a good laugh about that. I'm sorry this writing is going sideways, but I've been picking raspberries all day, so I'm lying on a sofa with my legs up . . .
 Much love
 Laughing Motorbike (alias Val)

Agnes to Valentine:

[Sept–Oct 1995]

My Dear Val,

Cheers! . . . I've actually managed to get pen to paper, if it's only for a short while. So much has happened that I wanted to chat to you about, but, no matter how much I wanted to, something always seemed to happen. We've had a long, hot, unbearable spell of weather which wasn't at all inducing of doing anything but sweat, drink, sweat, then eat a bit, sweat, and sleep! Life gets tedious don't it. Now there is a water shortage. My left leg has broken out in ulcers again which entails nurses coming Mondays, Wednesdays and Fridays to dress them. Then my stomach started playing up and I treated myself to a bottle of brandy, and I'm glad to say I'm much better. Margaretta phoned me and I told her about my brandy. I was then surprised when she phoned me again the following day to see if the B had worked . . .

Here I am again, two days later. I have a tray that rests on my knee to write and to eat, next to a glass topped table which is the home of a thousand and one things: my telephone, my nebuliser, diary, pills, pens, scissors and numerous letters and photographs, one of them Tamsy and the next one is Vicky. The pride of place goes to a lady called Valentine Morche. You are just about one foot away from the hand that is writing this. So you are constantly looking at me.

I wish you could have been here when we welders had our get-together. It was great seeing them again . . . The years just seemed to drop away. Apart from looking older, Emily and Ethel seemed very much the same, but Alice was very crippled walking, although she was still the quiet person she always was, and her features were very recognisable still, although she was 85 last January . . . Emily baked a lovely chocolate cake with about 1 inch of cream, Ethel brought home-baked ginger biscuits, scones and home-made jam and Margaretta and myself supplied the Champagne . . .

God Bless you Val, keep well and happy.

Lady Leonora XXX

Notes

1. See Sheridan, D. (1990), 'Ambivalent Memories: Women and the 1939–45 War in Britain', *Oral History* (Spring 1990): 32–40, for an analysis of the relatively narrow range of images that dominate popular memory of women's role during the war, including 'Rosie the Riveter'.
2. I refer to the letter writers and to Valentine from here on by their first names since this was how I addressed them in conversation.
3. The phrase 'blatancy and boom' comes from Woolf, V. (1940), 'The Humane Art', *New Statesman and Nation*: 726.
4. The Registration of Employment Act of March 1941, by which people could be directed towards essential war work, only applied to unmarried women between the ages of 20 and 21. This didn't produce the numbers of women hoped for, despite a massive advertising campaign, and the age limit was extended to 30, then 41, and eventually to all women between the ages of 18 and 50 (Waller, J. and M. Vaughan-Rees (1987), *Women in Wartime: The Role of Women's Magazines 1939–1945*, London, Macdonald). The National Service Number 2 Act of December 1941, which allowed women to be called up into the Women's Auxiliary Forces, also increased the flow of women into industry (Smith, H. L., ed. (1986), *War and Social Change: British Society in the Second World War*, Manchester, Eng., Manchester UP).
5. Castle, E. and A. Hargate (20 Jan 1989), personal interview with Penny Summerfield, Huddersfield.
6. The Brown foundry in Penistone then employed about 60 women as core-makers. A 'core', made from sand, is the inside shape of a mould used for casting metal.
7. Castle, E. and A. Hargate (20 Jan 1989), personal interview with Penny Summerfield, Huddersfield.
8. Helme, A. (20 Jan 1989), personal interview with Penny Summerfield, Huddersfield.
9. Varley, H. (20 Jan 1989), personal interview with Penny Summerfield, Huddersfield.
10. Baines, J. and D. Roebuck (13 Dec 1995), personal interview, Barnsley.

11. Ibid.

12. Varley, H. (20 Jan 1989), personal interview with Penny Summerfield, Huddersfield.

13. Morche, V. (10 June 1995), personal interview, Naramata, BC, Canada.

14. I have been unable to find anything out about Jenny, who left the job early and did not keep in touch with the rest of the women.

15. Morche, V. (10 June 1995), personal interview, Naramata, BC, Canada.

16. Buckley, S. (24 July 1996), personal interview, London.

17. Morche, V. (10 June 1995), personal interview, Naramata, BC, Canada.

18. Ibid.

19. Helme, A. (2 May 1995), personal interview, Huddersfield.

20. The diary was written for Mass-Observation, described in the Epilogue. She kept the diary from August 1939 until 1941, unfortunately stopping before the period when she trained the letter writers.

21. Morche, V. (10 June 1995), personal interview, Naramata, BC, Canada.

22. Penny Summerfield has also quoted this passage in Summerfield, P. and G. Braybon (1987), *Out of the Cage: Women's Experiences in Two World Wars*, London, Pandora. Dorothy Sheridan has also reprinted excerpts of the letter collection in Sheridan, D., ed. (1991), *Wartime Women: A Mass-Observation Anthology, the Experiences of Women at War*, London, Mandarin.

23. This was cutting sheet metal using a large gas-powered machine (see inset photograph). Emily and Amy were given this to do when they arrived at Hopkinsons (earlier than the others). According to Emily, they taught themselves how to use the machine.

24. The other principal kind of welding is oxyacetylene welding, in which a gas-fired flame is used. This method involves both hands, one hand directing the flame, the other feeding the metal rod down on to the object to be welded (as shown on the book cover). Oxyacetylene welding can be used for smaller jobs, whereas electric arc welding is solely used in heavy industry.

25. Morche, V. (10 June 1995), personal interview, Naramata, BC, Canada.

26. Helme, A. (2 May 1995), personal interview, Huddersfield.

27. Morche, V. (3 July 1996), letter to Anne Nyssen and the editor.

28. Ibid.

29. Baines, J. and D. Roebuck (13 Dec 1995), personal interview, Barnsley.

30. Helme, A. (20 Jan 1989), personal interview with Penny Summerfield, Huddersfield.
31. Castle, E. and A. Hargate (20 Jan 1989), personal interview with Penny Summerfield, Huddersfield.
32. Valentine says that she herself never had a medical test. Morche, V. (3 July 1996), letter to Anne Nyssen and the author.
33. Penny Summerfield notes that it is difficult to get an accurate figure for the number of women who continued in paid work after marriage during this period, since so many concealed their status from their employers due to the marriage bar. Summerfield, P. (1984), *Women Workers in the Second World War: Production and Patriarchy in Conflict*, London, Croom Helm.
34. British Restaurants were canteens run by local authorities, at first for those who had suffered air raids, and then to provide people with nourishing, unrationed food.
35. The Woman Power Committee, established in 1940, pressurised the Ministry of Labour to accept the need for special consideration of women's position, and measures to direct women's place in the war economy.
36. See Penny Summerfield's detailed study of the struggle between the Ministry of Labour on the one hand, representing the interests of production, and the Ministries of Health, and Food on the other, which believed that a woman's place was in the home and that organised child care, shopping and other schemes were unwanted by women themselves. Summerfield, P. (1984), *Women Workers in the Second World War: Production and Patriarchy in Conflict*, London, Croom Helm. She describes the members of the Women's Consultative Committee, established to advise the Ministry of Labour on the registration and conscription of women, as 'the architects of compromise between the pressure of war for women's labour, conventional expectations about women's work at home and the voluntary principle, in the context of recruitment'. Ruth Milkman, Sonya Michel and Alice Kessler-Harris have written on parallel compromises in US policies towards women workers. Kessler-Harris, A. (1982), *Out to Work: A History of Wage-Earning Women in the US*, Oxford, Oxford UP. Michel, S. (1987), 'American Women and the Discourse of the Democratic Family in World War II', *Behind the Lines: Gender and the Two World Wars*, M. R. Higonnet, J. Jenson, S. Michel and M. C. Weitz, New Haven, CT, Yale UP. Milkman, R. (1987), 'American Women and Industrial Unionism during World War II', ibid.
37. 'The numbers of women in arms production have grown as electronics has become the technological basis for modern weaponry. But they form a ghetto within that industry, a ghetto of wirers, winders, and

circuit assemblers . . . In Lucas Aerospace, for example, over 80 per cent of the workforce are highly skilled, both on the shop floor and in the drawing offices and design rooms. This 80 per cent is almost entirely male. Among the remaining 20 per cent of unskilled or semi-skilled workers are two groups of women.' Wainwright, H. (1983), 'The Women Who Wire Up the Weapons: Workers in Armament Factories', *Over Our Dead Bodies: Women Against the Bomb*, D. Thompson, London, Virago: 136–45. In the United States as a whole, approximately two-thirds of high-tech operatives are women, one-fourth of whom are black, Hispanic, Asian or Native-American. Enloe, C. (1988). *Does Khaki Become You? The Militarization of Women's Lives*, London, Pandora. Enloe's chapter 'Rosie the Riveter' is an excellent discussion of the military's exploitation of women in munitions work from the American Civil War to the present day.

38. Varley, H. (20 Jan 1989), personal interview with Penny Summerfield, Huddersfield.

39. This figure is according to Amy and Emily Castle, E. and A. Hargate (20 Jan 1989), personal interview with Penny Summerfield, Huddersfield, Mass-Observation Archive, Eng. However, Amy says in Letter 27 that 'I have had 7/7 off again for Income Tax and Marflit does not seem to be doing anything about it I have drawn three pounds this week for working 58 hours and the others have £2.15.0 for 48 so dont you think there ought to be an alteration I am getting between 900 and 1000 plates out a week.' Amy tells Valentine in Letter 21 that her hours are 7.30 a.m. to 7.00 p.m., and to 4.30 p.m. on a Saturday. Valentine considers that 'welders weren't particularly well paid then – I got £1-5s a day for teaching, that was pretty good then.' Morche, V. (3 July 1996), letter to Anne Nyssen and the author.

40. Castle, E. and A. Hargate (20 Jan 1989), personal interview with Penny Summerfield, Huddersfield.

41. Morche, V. (10 June 1995), personal interview, Naramata, BC, Canada.

42. Baines, J. and D. Roebuck (13 Dec 1995), personal interview, Barnsley.

43. Amy writes in early September, 'We are very well in with the men now. Emily was cutting one of them his hair on Friday. She made a good job of it too.' (Letter 28)

44. Varley, H. (20 Jan 1989), personal interview with Penny Summerfield, Huddersfield.

45. Anthony was the grand-niece of the famous American nineteenth-century feminist.

46. Such relief could take the form, she suggests, of 'decent recreation for the children, adequate feeding for the family at low cost to save the mother an 80 hour week made up of 48 hours at the plant and

32 hours in the kitchen, housekeeping aides who will see to the care of children taken sick' (9).

47. It has been calculated that between 1939 and 1949 the number of illegitimate births in the United Kingdom increased from 5·5 per thousand to 16·1 per thousand and the number of cases of venereal disease in Britain rose by 200 per cent during the first two years of the Second World War but then declined to below pre-war levels, after campaigns by the Ministry of Health and military authorities. An estimated 20,000 British women married men from Commonwealth countries, and 60,000 British women and 15,000 Australian women married American GIs in the war. (Agnes's description of meeting a black GI suggests the ingrained racism of the time, but also a typically white British naïveté that often meant the British were less hostile than the white Americans, from whom black soldiers were segregated.) After a sharp rise in 1939–40, the annual rate of marriages declined in Britain during the Second World War to below that in 1938. Divorces in Britain rose steeply during the war: there were 9,970 in 1938, but by 1947, after a change in the law, the number had increased to 47,041. The 'Forces Sweethearts' Exhibition, London, Imperial War Museum (1993).

48. Varley, H. (20 Jan 1989), personal interview with Penny Summerfield, Huddersfield.

49. Baines, J. and D. Roebuck (13 Dec 1995), personal interview, Barnsley.

50. Helme, A. (20 Jan 1989), personal interview with Penny Summerfield, Huddersfield.

51. In a recent letter to me, Valentine commented that, 'I hadn't at the time, thought anything about "Laughing Motorbike", other than it was one of Agnes's picturesque & extraordinary phrases. So I have just tried out my laugh (nobody being within earshot). And true enough, it's just like an oldfashioned motorbike starting up. No Harley Davidson – '. Morche, V. (16 Aug 1995), letter to the author.

52. 'Emily and I [Amy] went straight up to see Nellie after we had rung you up, and I regret to say she is ill in bed, but we had not time to go upstairs to see her as you know it was 12-50 when we left the phone box, so we are going up again tomorrow' (Letter 20).

53. The women shared an ethnic and religious background as white Christian northerners, but this was a passive rather than an active condition of their friendship. Valentine in some senses deliberately rejected this 'background' in her marriage to a Czech refugee, emigration to Canada after the war, and her later interest in non-Western and native Canadian spiritualities.

54. However, as Marilyn Lake has astutely argued in the Australian context, the fact that marriage and motherhood were still seen as the

final 'career' for a woman, should not obscure the changing meanings of these institutions themselves. She points out that the cult of both marriage and family at the end of the war was defined by a new discourse of heterosexual pleasure that included recognition of women as actively desiring subjects. Her study also interestingly uses (Australian) women's letters and diaries as evidence for this. See Lake, M. (1996), 'Female Desires: The Meaning of World War II', *Feminism and History*, J. W. Scott, Oxford, Oxford UP: 429–52.

55. 'The guide' may refer to Emily, who until then had worked with Amy at work and with whom she was very close. The letter informs Valentine that the two of them had just been put on different shifts.

56. Morche, V. (10 June 1995), personal interview, Naramata, BC, Canada.

57. Helme, A. (2 May 1995), personal interview, Huddersfield.

58. As Spacks also observes, 'Given its lack of immediate modification and response, written gossip can never correspond precisely to the oral form it in some respects mimics.' Spacks, P. M. (1986), *Gossip*, Chicago, U of Chicago P.

59. It should be noted that these letters are not part of the Mass-Observation Archive's collection, but have been privately lent to me by Agnes's son, John Helme.

60. Helme, A. (22 Aug 1942), letter to Jack Helme, private collection of John Helme.

61. There are, however, sporadic references to raids on Sheffield, one of which from Amy is intriguingly unconcerned about Valentine's safety: 'I knew you would be feeling lonely without the mob, but believe me, we would have been home this week in any case. Now the raids have started again, we should not have stopped there' (Letter 23). Nellie also asks: 'Have you had the Sirens? We were up last Thursday, but Aunty was over for a few weeks' rest, from Sunderland. They have been in it awful. Her House was hit, she looks ill, however she has gone back' (Letter 50). It is also notable that they all did fire-watching and air-raid duty at points, including Valentine.

62. A letter from Emily also confesses what cannot be said to her fiancé, who had been a German prisoner-of-war since 1940: 'I have had two letters this week, & he seems to be alright . . . he also told me not to be a land girl, he doesn't know what I am really doing, still its better that way, he has enough worries as it is' (Letter 40). Equally, men writing to women back home often censored their letters as rigorously as any official, sticking to sentimental themes of home-sickness rather than descriptions of what they were doing or describing less 'manly' emotions such as fear or bitterness. Valentine commented in a letter to me that: 'I thought that it went well for Agnes's integrity that she criticised Jack's overwhelming "dears & darlings". He used

"darling" like a comma. But I suppose it came from his heart & he couldn't think of anything else to fill his letter with, because he only mentions what he & the boys are doing, but nothing about thoughts or ideas'. Morche, V. (3 July 1996), letter to the author.

63. It has been suggested that this was particularly characteristic of Second World War culture, because the new styles of 'total' war broke down the opposition between 'fighting men' and 'protected women' that so many men in the First World War had found impossible to bridge. Of course, the large-scale separation of the sexes and creation of single-sex groups in the services, provides pockets for some to explore identities based around their own sex. Lilian Faderman, for example, has shown that the 1940s saw the emergence of a strong lesbian sub-culture. See Faderman, L. (1992), *Odd Girls and Twilight Lovers: A History of Lesbian Life in Twentieth-Century America*, Harmondsworth, Penguin. But largely war can only reinforce conservative notions of sexual role, newly imbued with the powerful nostalgia for 'before the war'. As Susan Hartmann argues, these are often cruelly put to the test when the war ends and couples are reunited to discover how very incompatible their war experiences have made them, particularly as they have exaggerated the oppositions between 'protected' women at home and 'heroic' men fighting or waiting it out at the Front. Hartmann, S. M. (1978), 'Prescriptions for Penelope: Literature on Women's Obligations to Returning World War II Veterans', *Women's Studies* 5: 223–39. The millions of letters that were written by both sides in an attempt to bridge these psychological as well as physical gulfs are interesting evidence of this, precisely because their ideals (although very often the stuff of creativity) so often didn't match the realities. See Jolly, M. (1996), *Everyday Letters and Literary Form: Correspondence from the Second World War*, doctoral thesis, University of Sussex.

64. A letter belongs to its recipient, although copyright belongs to its author.

65. Mass-Observation became a limited company in 1949. It wound down its activities during the 1950s and lay dormant until 1975 when it was re-established as an Archive. Since 1981 it has been operating at the University of Sussex, where it continues to collect reports from self-nominated 'Mass-Observers'.

66. Hargate, A. (20 Jan 1989), personal interview with Penny Summerfield, Huddersfield.

67. Castle, E. (14 Sept 1995), personal interview, Huddersfield. In her interview with Penny Summerfield Emily similarly said, 'I just wrote the one letter when we left, a sort of a thank you letter. That's all I ever wrote. Because to me that was just an interlude in my life to get over with, you know.' Castle, E. and A. Hargate (20 Jan 1989),

personal interview with Penny Summerfield, Huddersfield, Mass-Observation Archive, Eng.

68. See Thomson, A. (1995), 'Memory as a Battlefield: Personal and Political Investments in the National Military Past', *Oral History Review*, 22 (2): 55–73, for a fascinating account of the different kinds of emotional and political 'investment' that can structure oral history interviews and texts, in his own case centring upon masculinity and military identity.

69. One of Agnes's poems to her son, John:

I longed to have a daughter when we were newly wed.
I didn't have a daughter, We had a son instead.
He wasn't very robust, his thread of life so fine
They said I couldn't rear him, that he never would be mine.

For years the doctors treated him, then gradually we see
A lovely – little boy, as sturdy as a tree.
From five to fifteen school days, how swiftly years do pass
I burst with pride the day he said 'I'm number one in class'.

He joined the Royal Navy and now my son's a man,
For he'll be twenty-one next year. It surely was God's plan
That I should have a son so fine, so thoughtful and so good
He's proved as good as much a blessing as any daughter could.

In twenty years he's grown a man of character and worth
Thank God I say for you dear Jack, thank God I gave you birth.

It is interesting, however, that the only poem that she appears to have written for the general public, sent in for a competition in a local newspaper, titled 'What I'd do if I won the pools in 1961', was much pithier, and indeed, won the 'Pick of Ten Thousand':

M'Lord – first I'd carefully – tend it
Then – oh! Gosh and golly, I'd – spend it
The drag of HP I should – end it
To deserving charities – send it.
The Hole of Discontent – mend it
The long road of happiness – wend it
There's one thing I would not do – lend it!
That's my case M'Lord, now please – defend it!

She got £10 for it.

70. There are also, of course, broader influences on people's versions of themselves, for example, the way that the war has become a discourse imbued with new right patriotism.
71. To some extent, the same process happened in my relationship with Dorothy Sheridan, the Mass-Observation Archivist, who was a constant reference in my research and had herself corresponded with the surviving welders.
72. Much of the work had already been done for me by Penny Summerfield and Dorothy Sheridan, who had sorted the letters chronologically, and Maud Pratt who had typed them.
73. Another subsidiary of David Brown which employed the women in Penistone.
74. Penny Summerfield.

Bibliography

Anthony, S. B., II (1943), *Out of the Kitchen, Into the War: Women's Winning Role in the Nation's Drama*, New York, Daye.

Bradley, L. V. (1944), 'Women at Work', *National Geographic* (August): 193–220.

Enloe, C. (1988), *Does Khaki Become You? The Militarization of Women's Lives*, London, Pandora.

Faderman, L. (1992), *Odd Girls and Twilight Lovers: A History of Lesbian Life in Twentieth-Century America*, Harmondsworth, Penguin.

Fussell, P. (1989), *Wartime: Understanding and Behaviour in the Second World War*, New York, Oxford UP.

Hartmann, S. M. (1978), 'Prescriptions for Penelope: Literature on Women's Obligations to Returning World War II Veterans', *Women's Studies* 5: 223–39.

Horowitz, Louise K. (1981), 'The Correspondence of Madame de Sévigné: Letters or Belles-Lettres?', *French Forum* 6: 13–27.

Hunt, A., ed. (1988), *Women and Paid Work: Issues of Equality*, Basingstoke, Macmillan.

Jolly, M. (1996), *Everyday Letters and Literary Form: Correspondence from the Second World War*, doctoral thesis, University of Sussex.

Kessler-Harris, A. (1982), *Out to Work: A History of Wage-Earning Women in the US*, Oxford, Oxford UP.

Lake, M. (1996), 'Female Desires: The Meaning of World War II', *Feminism and History*, J. W. Scott, Oxford, Oxford UP: 429–52.

Michel, S. (1987), 'American Women and the Discourse of the Democratic Family in World War II', *Behind the Lines: Gender and the Two World Wars*, M. R. Higonnet, J. Jenson, S. Michel and M. C. Weitz, New Haven, CT, Yale UP.

Milkman, R. (1987), 'American Women and Industrial Unionism during World War II', *Behind the Lines: Gender and the Two World Wars*, M. R. Higonnet, J. Jenson, S. Michel and M. C. Weitz, New Haven, CT, Yale UP.

Phillips, A. (1987), *Divided Loyalties: Dilemmas of Sex and Class*, London, Virago.

Sheridan, D. (1990), 'Ambivalent Memories: Women and the 1939–45 War in Britain', *Oral History* (Spring): 32–40.

Sheridan, D., ed. (1991), *Wartime Women: A Mass-Observation Anthology, the Experiences of Women at War*, London, Mandarin.

Smith, H. L., ed. (1986), *War and Social Change: British Society in the Second World War*, Manchester, Eng., Manchester UP.

Spacks, P. M. (1986), *Gossip*, Chicago, U of Chicago P.

Summerfield, P. (1984), *Women Workers in the Second World War: Production and Patriarchy in Conflict*, London, Croom Helm.

Summerfield, P. and G. Braybon (1987), *Out of the Cage: Women's Experiences in Two World Wars*, London, Pandora.

Thomson, A. (1995), 'Memory as a Battlefield: Personal and Political Investments in the National Military Past', *Oral History Review* 22(2): 55–73.

Wainwright, H. (1983), 'The Women Who Wire Up the Weapons: Workers in Armament Factories', *Over Our Dead Bodies: Women Against the Bomb*, D. Thompson, London, Virago: 136–45.

Waller, J. and M. Vaughan-Rees (1987), *Women in Wartime: The Role of Women's Magazines 1939–1945*, London, Macdonald.

Woolf, V. (1940), 'The Humane Art', *New Statesman and Nation*: 726.

Index

Also available from Scarlet Press

The Midwife's Tale
An oral history from handywoman to professional midwife

Nicky Leap and Billie Hunter

Widely acclaimed, *The Midwife's Tale* is the hitherto untold story of the way the role of the working-class handywoman was usurped by the professional midwife. Authors Nicky Leap and Billie Hunter have created from hundreds of hours of interviews with handywomen, midwives and mothers, a book that challenges assumptions about home birth and the midwifery profession. It provides a detailed insight into women's attitudes to and experiences of childbirth from the early twentieth century to the foundation of the NHS in 1948.

'I highly recommend this book as a welcome addition to the library of anyone interested in women's health and social issues, midwifery, feminist history, or the art of oral interviewing and research. It's hard to set this book down, once you start to read it! *Journal of Human Lactation*

' ... fascinating oral history of midwifery pre-NHS Britain.' *Oral History Journal*

'These are delightful and inspiring accounts from both midwives and the mothers who used midwives at their birth ...' *Birth Magazine*

'It is excellent reading for any nurse midwife, physician or women's study enthusiast.' *Journal of Nurse-Midwifery*

ISBN 1 85727 041 X
248pp, 20 b/w illustrations

In a League of Their Own!
The Dick, Kerr Ladies Football Club

Gail Newsham

The story of the Dick, Kerr Ladies football team cannot be forgotten. Formed during the First World War to raise money for charity, they were not only unbeatable but the public loved them. At Goodison Park, Everton, on Boxing Day 1920, 53,000 paid to see them play and over the years hundreds of thousands watched them both here and abroad. In 1921 the FA banned women from playing on FA affiliated pitches. For the next 40 years Dick, Kerr's Ladies kept the women's game alive and when they folded in 1965 they had raised in the region of £175,000 for charity.

In a League of Their Own! charts the team's voyage through the years, profiles the great pioneering players, and brings to light the financial mismanagement which laid a shadow of their success. Their remarkable story gives an invaluable insight into the early days of women's football.

'Triumph, glory, betrayal and prejudice are all intriguing, winning features of *In a League of Their Own!* but Gail Newsham has also uncovered the spirit and rare soccer talent which made Dick, Kerr Ladies Football Club the best in the world.' *Preston Citizen*

'It is a story of unparalleled sporting achievement, a struggle again prejudice and financial skullduggery.' *Blackpool Evening Gazette*

ISBN 1 85727 029 0
160pp, 31 b/w illustrations